Python Programming

A Comprehensive Smart Approach for Total Beginners to Learn Python Language Using Best Practices and Advanced Features

By: Ethem Mining

Copyright © 2019 – All rights reserved.

No part of this publication may be reproduced, duplicated or transmitted in any form or by any means, electronic, mechanical, scanning, photocopying, recording or otherwise without prior written permission from the publisher. All rights reserved.

The information provided herein is stated to be truthful and consistent in that any liability, regarding inattention or otherwise, by any usage or abuse of any policies, processes or directions contained within is the solitary and complete responsibility of the recipient reader. Under no circumstances will any legal liability or blame be held against the publisher for any reparation, damages or monetary loss due to the information herein, either directly or indirectly.

Legal Notice.

This book is copyright protected. This is only for personal use. You cannot amend, distribute, sell, quote, use or paraphrase any part of the content within this book without the consent of the author or copyright owner. Legal action will be pursued if this is breached.

Disclaimer Notice.

Please note the information contained within this document is for educational and entertainment purposes only. This book not intended to be a substitute for medical advice. Please consult your health care provider for medical advice and treatment.

Table of Contents

Introduction

Chapter 1: What You Need to Know Before You Start

    What is Python? 12
    What can you develop with Python? 17
    How to install Python in your Operating System? ... 21
    You first 'Hello World' Program 25

Chapter 2: Variables in Python

    What is a variable? 29
    How to declare, re-declare, and delete variables?... 31
    What are the local and global variables? 36

Chapter 3: Python data objects

    What are the Python data objects? 43
    Number Data Object in Python 46
    String Data Object in Python 58
    List data object in Python 65

Dictionary data object in Python 74

Tuples data object in Python 85

Chapter 4: Python Operators

Python Statements Syntax 93

Syntax rules in Python 108

Python If Test and Its Variations 113

Loops in Python (while and for loop) 120

Continue, Break and Pass Statements with Python Loops 131

Python Exceptions 144

Chapter 5: Functions in Python

Function Utilities in Programming 155

Function Concept, Declaration and Calling in Python 157

Function Expressions, Arguments, and Returned outputs 163

Chapter 6: Modules in Python

Modules Concept and Utility Within Python 170
How to Import a Module 175
How to write and use a module in Python? 181

Chapter 7: Python Debugging

What is debugging? 196
Python Debugger Commands 199

Chapter 8: Files in Python

Reading and writing files in Python 217
Example File Processing in Python 221

Conclusion

Introduction

This book is designed to be a step-by-step guide for total beginners to learn to program with Python. This book covers all the basics of Python programming languages from the data object types to debugging methods for large programs. This book has eight chapters where each chapter discusses a specific topic with code examples provided. The present book is structured as follows.

The first chapter of this book provides the big picture of Python programming language, its features as well as its strengths. It also presents the necessary tools in order to start using Python languages and be able to test the examples provided in the book.

The second chapter provides a general idea of what is a variable in Python, how to declare a variable as well as the difference between global and local variables.

Chapter three of this book presents the set of a built-in data object in Python. It also presents the necessary functions and methods to process these data object type. Chapter four presents first the basics of Python syntax. Although Python is designed as readable with an easy syntax, there are some basic rules to follow which are given in this chapter. This chapter presents the if test and loops syntax and Python exceptions that are used to process data objects that were presented in chapter three.

Chapters five and six discuss how to make your code and scripts more general, reusable, and sharable with other programmers via the notion of functions and modules. Chapter five is dedicated to functions and chapter 6 is dedicated to modules.

Chapter seven of this book is dedicated to debugging with Python. It is common among programmers to use debugging in order to fix any errors in their programs after they are developed. This chapter presents the Python debugger and its commands.

Finally, chapter eight covers processing files with Python. Files are important whether to read from or to write processed data. Writing and reading of the files will also be explained in this chapter.

Plenty of books on this subject are available in the market and we thank you for choosing this one. This book was made with care to make it a useful Python basic book for total beginners that wish to learn to program with Python.

Chapter 1: What You Need to Know Before You Start

The aim of this chapter is to get you started with Python and explain the basics behind Python programming. In fact, this chapter provides you with basics that you need to know before you start learning the basic Python programming language. In this chapter, we discuss what is Python and the Python features that make it an attractive programming language for large domain applications. We also present how you can download and install Python according to your Operating System. We also expose ways on how to launch and execute Python code. Of course, like in any programming language, we will show you how to develop your first famous program 'Hello World'. We won't actually start coding until the next chapters. We expose here just some examples so you can get the general picture behind Python.

What is Python?

Python is a programming language that has several features that makes it very attractive to programmers and developers. First of all, Python is a free programming language which means it is available for anybody. Python is also an open-source language which means you can contribute to the source code if you wish. In fact, Python is a language that is supported by a community that gathers its effort through the internet to improve this language. Python is a language that belongs to the category of high-level languages.

This implies that Python does not require compiling like other languages such as C or C++, Fortran, and so on. It implies also that the syntax of Python is very easy to use and learn. These features make Python programs to be easily developed, interpreted, and maintained at low cost. Therefore, it allows sharing and collaborating to develop applications based on Python very efficient.

Being an easy syntax and high-level programming language does not mean that Python is a very slow programming language. In fact, Python is considered a very competitive and productive language. When compared to other programming languages that are low-level and known to be fast, a Python script can be 3rd or 5th size of a similar script developed with C++ or Java. In addition to requiring less typing and debugging, Python does not require compiling. Once a Python script is developed, it can be run directly without additional steps of compiling or linking to other tools or libraries.

Another feature that makes Python an interesting programming language is its portability.

Python language is portable and can be run in any Operating environment or system without any changes. The same Python code can be run on Windows, UNIX / LINUX, Mac, on large servers, Android, or iOs tablets. Even graphical user interface applications can be developed to be portable using options that are supported in Python.

Different from other languages like Java or C, Python offers a dynamic typing environment. Variables in Python can be used without declaration or type specification prior to use. Any variable can be used without specifying its type which makes developing codes very straight forward.

A very attractive feature of Python is the libraries that come with it. These libraries, also called packages, are a set of code tools that allows performing basic and common tasks. Python comes with a default library called the standard library which includes a set of modules like the math module for mathematical and numerical programming. Moreover, Python supports using other libraries developed by third parties.

There is a wide range of third parties' packages that are available online and allows using advanced tools for a specific domain (e.g. Numpy library for Numerical programming with Python, Pandas, Matplotlib for developing figures and so on). Hence, when coding with Python language, you have access to a wide set of tools and pre-coded and built-in objects that can be easily used. You never start from scratch because there is a high chance that the function you want to use was already coded and made available for use by anybody.

Python can be considered as a hybrid language in the context that it allows integrating and to be integrated with other programming languages. For instance, you can use pre-coded or compiled libraries that are written in C or C++ within Python. You can also call Python codes from scripts that are written in C or C++.

Overall, If you opt for Python as a language to develop your applications, you get the following benefits:
1) easy syntax and less typing;
2) a program that is fast to execute;
3) a program that is portable and usable within any operating system;

4) a program that is easily maintained and well organized;

5) never start from scratch with access to a wide variety of packages and codes ready to be used;

6) integrated components that allow running codes in C, C++, or any other language to speed up execution of parts of the code.

These are some characteristics and benefits of using Python as a language for programming.

What can you develop with Python?

Given the strong features of Python, this programming language can be used to develop a wide range of applications from stand-alone scripts, to graphical user interface applications or integrated programming. In fact, Python is considered as a scripting language to develop easy programs given its readability and easy syntax. However, because it evolved to be also an object-oriented programming language, Python has similar characteristics as the low-level object-oriented languages such as C++. This implies that you can develop modules and classes with Python that benefits from multiple inheritances, polymorphism, and operator overloading. A class is the main notion in object-oriented programming that allows defining an object with its attributes and methods to handle it. So, Python offers the ability to define and develop modular applications.

Python also supports shell script programming that allows developing system programs. Indeed, Python programs are usable on any platform without change, so it is very suitable for shell script programming.

These shell scripts are typically used to fetch files, directories, set/change paths, or execute and launch other programs. The POSIX bindings available among the Python standard library support all tools of the Operating system that includes the environment variables, files, filename expansions, command-line arguments, and much more. These tools can be easily handled within Python scripts for shell scripting programming.

Graphical user interface (GUI) applications can be easily developed with Python using the package Tkinter. This library supports graphical user development that is compatible with any operating system, LINUX/UNIX, Mac, and Windows, with no change required.

Python also supports developing internet scripts. A standard Internet module is included in the standard library that comes with Python. This module allows developing scripts that perform networking jobs in the server and in the client. You can develop codes that get information from a server or transfer files via FTP. It allows also processing XML files, and emails (i.e. send, receive or parse).

It allows developing scripts that sort and search internet pages via URL. In addition, you can perform Internet programming where you can develop scripts to generate HTML files and websites.

Python can be used as glue programming that launches or runs other programs. For instance, you can easily test libraries written in C or C++ using Python scripts for rapid execution and evaluation.

Python supports numerical and engineering programming, data analysis, and image processing through its libraries Pandas, NumPy, and Matplotlib. Other libraries are available in particular for data analysis. Python also supports performing database programming. It offers tools to read, save, and perform all common tasks on the database. Moreover, it supports an interface that allows using the traditional syntax of MySQL, Oracle, Sybase, ODBC, or Informix for those who prefer using them.

Those were examples of what you can develop with Python programming language.

In general, you can develop anything you want given the panoply of tools and libraries that are available in Python. In addition, Python is a very popular and widely used language in a wide range of applications. Hence, it is always updated and new tools and third parties' libraries are always developed and made available for the public. In addition, Python has a very strong community to help resolve any issues with the language.

Now that you are familiar with Python features and what can you do with Python, let's see how Python can be installed on any Operating System.

How to install Python in your Operating System?

Python is a free programming language that can be downloaded from Python's official website www.Python.org. Python is available as software that includes the standard libraries and the interpreter. The latter is a program in the form of an executable that works, as its name suggests, as an interpreter or translator to the hardware of the machine. Its purpose is to interpret Python codes into a binary form that the machine hardware is able to process. After downloading and installing Python on your machine, several components will be automatically generated that includes the interpreter as executable and the standard library of Python.

If you have Linux or Mac OS, Python might be already available on your operating system. To check if Python is already available, you can type in a prompt shell 'Python'. This should return a '>>>' if Python is available, otherwise, it will display an error message that Python is not recognized as a command line.

Another way to check if Python is available in Linux is to search Python manually in the folders 'usr/local/bin'or '/usr/bin'. If it isn't already available on your LINUX environment, you can download Python for Linux from the Python official website. It comes in several rpm files that can be zipped easily. Python should then be compiled from the source code contained in the zipped directory using the make command and running the config. This should set automatically the configuration of Python in your system. Python generally comes with a README file that explains the instructions to follow in order to install Python.

On Mac OS, Python 2.0 is typically already installed, and basically, you don't have to install or configure anything. However, you can always install the latest version of Python, which is version 3, that is considered the most up to date. Before installing Python, you might need to install OSX-GCC which can be downloaded using Xcode. If you already have Xcode installed, then you don't need to install the GCC. Then you need to install Homebrew. To do so, you need to launch your OS prompt shell, then execute:

```
$ /usr/bin/ruby -e "$(curl -fsSL
https://raw.githubusercontent.com/Homebrew/install/
master/install)"
```

Once Homebrew is installed, you can add it to your path environment variable as follows:

```
export PATH = /usr/local/bin:/usr/local/sbin:$PATH
```

Now, you are ready to install Python using the following command:

```
$ brew install Python
```

If you are using a Windows Operating System, installing Python is very straightforward. You can download from the Python official website the appropriate version for Windows. The downloaded folder is a zipped directory that comes as a self-installer.

You unzip the folder and launch the executable. Then in the installer window, you can click Yes for every window to install Python with the default settings. This should install Python with documentation, graphical user support, an IDLE development as well as the necessary settings you would need to run Python scripts appropriately. After the installation is finished, Python will figure in the start menu among the programs.

Now that you know how to install Python on your machine, we are going to see how you can run Python scripts and, of course, how to make your first program that displays 'Hello World'.

You first 'Hello World' Program

Python can be started from a command line through the prompt of your Operating System. You simply type 'Python' in the prompt. In Windows, for example, this can be done in the WINDOWS DOS console. After running 'Python' command to launch Python interpreter in the prompt, it displays the following 2 Lines:

> C:\Users***>Python
> Python 3.7.1 (default, Dec 10 2018, 22:54:23) [MSC v.1915 64 bit (AMD64)] :: Anaconda, Inc. on win32
> Type "help", "copyright", "credits" or "license" for more information.
> >>>

Basically, it displays the information about the Python version installed and currently launched and commands to get more information. When the prompt displays '>>>', it means that it is ready to execute Python code. To exit Python from the prompt shell on Windows, you can type Ctrl-Z. On Linux or Unix environments, you can use Ctrl-D.

Now, we are going to develop and execute your first 'Hello World' program. After you have launched Python in your prompt shell, you can run the following command:

>>> print ('Hello World')
Hello World

The 'print' command is a function that tells Python to display anything between the parenthesis. We will go through built-in functions in the next chapters. Note here that we are working in an interactive session. Everything that we run is lost once the prompt shell is exited. The code that we type is executed instantly when we hit Enter but lost after ending the session. This is a good way to practice and test quickly some commands. However, it is best suited to save the code somewhere and run it every time you need it. This should save the time of re-writing a script whenever you need it. To do so, you can use a script Editor like Notepad++ to develop and write the script. Then the script should be saved in a file with '.py' extension.

This would allow Python to recognize and read the scripts that are written in the file as Python script. Now, you can write in a text editor the following commands:

>   print ('Hello World')
>   print ('\n Executing my first Python program')

You can save the file as Hello.py. Now, to run this code, you have to launch your operating system prompt shell, then call Python and pass as argument the name of the script we just developed. For instance, on Windows you would type in WINDOWS DOS console:

>   C:\Users***>Python Hello.py
>   Hello World
>   Executing my first Python program

Note that if in the prompt shell the directory where your Python file is saved is different from your working directory, you should pass as an argument to Python the entire path of your script file like follows:

C:\Users***> Python path_script/Hello.py.

In the second print of this example, we added '\n'; this tells Python to go into the following line.

Chapter 2: Variables in Python

This chapter discusses the Variables in Python. We will start with a definition of what a variable is in Python. Then, we will see how to declare and re-declare variables. We will also see the local and global variables and the difference between these two variables.

What is a variable?

A variable is typically a reserved memory to a saved value on your machine. According to the data type to be stored in a variable, a Python interpreter will allocate memory to save the variable. In Python, variables do not have to be explicitly declared before they are used. In other words, you don't need to define the type or size of any variable before it is used in Python. Basically, Python does not allocate any memory for variables prior to their use. Variables are defined and memory is allocated instantaneously when the variable is used.

In Python, variables are objects that can be a number, string, list, dictionary, tuple, or a file. We will explain in detail each data object type in the next chapter. For the sake of simplicity and to explain variables and how to declare and manipulate them in this chapter, we will consider the basic data object number and strings. A number object type can be, for instance, an integer or a decimal.

Before going into how to declare and assign values to variables, there are some rules that should be followed to name a variable or a data object in Python. We cover more of this topic in chapter 4 of this book. First of all, only alpha-numeric characters and underscores can be used to name a Python variable. A variable name cannot start with a numeric. For instance, a variable name can be something like A_20. But 20_A cannot be used as a name for a variable. In Python, variables are case sensitive. For instance, PRICE, price, and Price are three different variables. We will cover more on variable names in Chapter 4 of this book.

How to declare, re-declare, and delete variables?

Remember that in Python, variables do not require any pre-allocation, type, or size specification prior to use. A variable is defined once a value is assigned to it. The equal operator '=' is the operator that assigns values to an object variable. The variable name is the left operand and the value to be stored in the variable is the right operand. For instance, we create the following variable:

```
>>> A = 200
>>> print (' The variable A is: ', A)
The variable A is: 200
```

Here we created a number variable. We can also declare or define several variables in a single statement as follows:

```
>>> A, B, C = 100, 200, 8
>>>print (' The variable A is: ', A)
>>> ('\n The variable B is: ', B)
>>> ('\n The variable C is: ', C)
The variable A is: 100
The variable B is: 200
The variable C is: 8
```

In this example, we declared three number variables in a single statement. We can also declare in a single statement several variables of different types as follows:

```
>>> A, B = 12, 'Price'
>>> print (' The variable A is: ', A)
>>> print ('\n The variable B is: ', B)
The variable A is: 12
The variable B is: Price
```

We can re-declare a variable by assigning a new value to the variable. For example:

```
>>> A = 2000
>>>print (' The variable A is: ', A)
The variable A is: 2000
>>> A = 400
>>>print (' The new value of the variable A is: ', A)
The new value of the variable A is: 400
```

We can also change the type of a declared variable by assigning a new type of data. For example, we can declare a variable as a number then we can change its value to a string.

```
>>> A = 100
>>>print (' The variable A is: ', A)
The variable A is: 100
>>> A = 'Date'
>>>print (' The new value of the variable A is: ', A)
The new value of the variable A is: Date
```

Variables in Python can be deleted using the function del. This function is used as followed:

```
>>> A = 100
>>> del A
```

Like assigning multiple variables, the function del can delete multiple variables as follows:

```
>>> A, B, C = 100, 200, 300
>>> del A, B, C
```

Now, if you want to access any variable, Python will throw an error message. For example, if you try displaying variable B:

```
>>> B
Traceback (most recent call last):
File "<stdin>", line 1, in <module>
NameError: name 'B' is not defined
```

Now, you have learned how to declare and re-declare and delete variables in Python. In the next section, we will see what is a local and global variable in Python.

What are the local and global variables?

Remember that in Python, functions and modules can be defined. Variables that are defined inside of these functions are called local variables. Global variables are all variables that are declared in the main script outside of the functions. The global variables can be used inside or outside a function even if they are not defined inside a function. For instance, let's consider the following code:

```
>>> def my_fct():
...        print ('The value of the global variable is:', A)
```

In the code above, we defined a function that displays the value stored in the variable A which is not defined inside the function. So, the variable A is a global variable. Now, we can declare a variable A and print its value by calling the function my_fct() we defined as follows:

```
>>> A = 100
>>> my_fct()
The value of the global variable is: 100
```

Now, let's see how can we change any global variable within a function. For example, we define a function that multiplies the value of the global variable:

```
>>> def my_fct():
...     A = A * 2
...     print (' The value of the variable is: ', A)
```

Now, after we define a variable and call the function my_fct() we defined, we get the following output:

```
>>> A = 1
>>> my_fct()
UnboundLocalError: local variable 'A' referenced before assignment
```

This code throws an error because Python is treating the variable 'A' as a local variable that is not defined inside the function. Therefore, Python cannot recognize it. To be able to change a global variable inside a function, we should use the global keyword.

The global keyword is a keyword in Python that enables changing a global variable outside of the current script and makes the changes in a local environment (i.e. inside a function). The global keyword has some rules that should be followed when it is used. The global keyword is used only to read and write (i.e. make changes) to a global variable within a function. Using the global keyword outside of a routine or a function does not have any effect. A global variable defined outside a function is, by default, a global variable and a variable declared inside a function is, by default, a local variable. In the previous example, to change the global variable 'A' inside the function my_fct(), we should add the following command into the function script: global A. So, the function script should be like follows:

```
>>> def my_fct():
...     global A
...     A = A * 2
...     print (' The value of the variable is: ', A)
```

Now, if you define a variable 'A' outside of the function my_fct() and call the function, we get the following output:

>>> A = 1
>>> my_fct()
The value of the variable is: 2

Note that the variable is changed also in the script not only inside the function. If we display the variable 'A' outside the function, the value is :

>>> print (' The value of the variable outside the function is: ', A)
The value of the variable outside the function is: 2

If a local variable is declared in a function and then the same variable is declared as a global variable outside a function, calling the function does not change the value of the global variable. To make it more explicit, let's see an example:

```
>>> def f():
...     V = 'Charles'
...     print ('The local variable is:', V)
>>> V = 'John'
>>> f()
The local variable is: Charles
>>> print ('The global variable is:', V)
The local variable is: John
```

Local variables are only accessed within the function. In a script, a local variable cannot be accessed from outside the function where it is defined. For instance, if we define a function as follows:

```
>>> def f1():
... var = 1
... print (' The local variable is:', var)
```

If we call the function we just defined, the output is as follows:

```
>>> f1()
The local variable is: 1
```

Python throws an error when we try to access the variable 'var' from outside the function as shown below:

```
>>> print(var)
Traceback (most recent call last):
File "<stdin>", line 1, in <module>
NameError: name 'var' is not defined
```

Chapter 3: Python data objects

In this chapter, we will cover the basic data objects in Python. We will also cover the operations that can be performed on these data objects and also how to manipulate them.

What are the Python data objects?

Python data objects are the variables in which save data that will be analyzed or processed. In Python, there are five major data objects types which are: number, strings, lists, dictionaries, and tuples. Numbers are the fundamental data type that also to store numeric variables. Strings in Python are a chain or a sequence of characters. Unlike other languages such as C, in Python, there is no character data object type to save a character singleton. Strings can be a single character or a sequence of characters. Lists are data structure in Python that allows saving items of different types.

In fact, strings are a list that contains only characters. However, lists provide a flexible way to save multiple data of different types in a single data object. Dictionary is another flexible data object that allows in Python to save data of different types in the same data object or variable. The main difference between lists and dictionaries is how the data is stored and how it is fetched. In lists, items are saved from left to right position and are indexed. Items in lists can be accessed using index or position. On the other hand, items in dictionaries are saved according to a key, meaning that items in dictionaries are not ordered and can be accessed using a key. Items in a dictionary are saved in a randomized way and the only way to access them is by key.

In Python, the function type() allows verifying variables types. This function takes as input a variable and returns the type of the variable passed as input. Let's some examples of applying this function.

```
>>> A = 200
>>> print ('Type of variable A is: ', type(A))
Type of variable A is: <class 'int'>
>>> A = 'chain of characters'
>>> print ('Type of variable A is: ', type(A))
Type of variable A is: <class 'str'>
>>> A = [1,'p', 300]
>>> print ('Type of variable A is: ', type(A))
Type of variable A is: <class 'list'>
```

In the first example, we defined the variable 'A' as an integer number, the type function returned as output class integer. In the second example, we declared the variable 'A' as a string, the type function returned a class string. Finally, in the third example, the variable 'A' is declared as a list and the function type returned a class list. Now that you know the different types of data objects in Python, in the next sections of this chapter, we will cover in detail each data type. Let's start with the most basic one, the number data type.

Number Data Object in Python

The number data object is the most basic data object that allows the processing of numeric variables in any programming language. This data object allows the processing quantity data. In Python, a number data object or variable can be an integer, a float number, or a complex number. Python also offers several functions that allow handling this data object. Python also supports normal integer, a long integer with unlimited precision. Basically, integers are a string of decimal digits that can be positive or negative. Float numbers can be a negative or positive number with a decimal point. Python supports the scientific representation of floating numbers with an exponent written with E or e indicating the power. Even though a number with exponent is an integer, Python considers it as a floating number and uses float-point math functions when performing mathematical operations such as addition, subtraction, or multiplication.

Python offers all basic mathematical functions and operators to process number variables.

The table below summarizes all comparison operators that can be used on number variables. Basically, these operators allow comparing between variables whether they are equal, or if the left operand is superior or inferior to the right operand.

Table 1: Comparison operators to be performed on number variables

Operator	Explanation
X > Y	X is strictly superior to Y
X >= Y	X superior or equal to Y
X < Y	X strictly inferior to Y
X <= Y	X inferior or equal to Y
X == Y	X is equal to Y
X != Y	X is different than Y

In the following table, we cover the logical operators that can be performed on number variables. These operators allow object comparison, whether two variables are true if a number variable belongs to other object data.

Table 2: Logical operators to be performed on number variables.

Operator	Explanation
X **and** Y	both X and Y should be true (i.e. Y is evaluated unless X is true)
X **or** Y	X or Y is true (i.e. Y is evaluated unless X is false)
not X	logical negation
X **is** Y	object comparison
X **is not** Y	object comparison
X **in**	X belonging to another object
X **not in**	X not belonging to another object
|	bitwise or
^	bitwise exclusive
&	bitwise and

The table below summarizes the mathematical operations that Python supports on number variables. These operations include addition, subtraction, multiplication, negation, and division.

Table 3: Mathematical operators to be performed on a number of variables.

Operator	Explanation
X + Y	X plus Y
X - Y	X minus Y
X // Y	X divided by Y
X % Y	The remainder of the division of X by Y
X * Y	X multiplied by Y
+ X	identity of X which equal to X
- X	negation of X
X ** Y	X power Y

Remember that when performing several mathematical operations in one single statement, the rules of mathematical operations applies. That being said, Python will always start by evaluating multiplication first, then it evaluates the other operations. For instance, if we consider the following statement Z = A * X + Y, Python will evaluate A * X then add the result to Y. If we want to specify a certain order of operations, let's say we want to evaluate first X + Y then multiply the result by A, then we should add parenthesis around

X + Y. To do so, the statement should be Z = A * (X + Y). Therefore, the results returned by Z = A * X + Y and Z = A * (X + Y) are very different. When adding parenthesis, Python evaluates first the expressions between parenthesis. Let's apply a real example of the two expressions given above.

```
>>> A = 4
>>> X = 5
>>> Y = 9
>>> Z = A * X + Y
>>> print ('Z = A * X + Y is:', Z)
Z = A * X + Y is: 29
>>> Z = A * (X + Y)
>>> print ('Z = A * (X + Y) is:', Z)
Z = A * (X + Y) is: 56
```

We can see from the example above that the first expression Z = A * X +Y returns 29 for A = 4, X = 5 and Y = 9. Python computes first A * X (i.e. 5 * 4) which is, in this case, 20 and adds Y (i.e. 9) to it which gives 29. For the second expression Z = A * (X + Y), Python evaluates first X + Y (i.e. 5 + 9) which is 14, then it multiplies it by A (i.e. 4) which gives 56.

Python supports evaluating multiple expressions in one single line and returns the results in a tuple. For instance, we can evaluate the two expressions A * X and Z +Y in one single line as follows:

```
>>> A = 4
>>> X = 5
>>> Y = 9
>>> Z = 56
>>> A * X, Z + Y
(20, 65)
```

As we have seen before, we can evaluate the two expressions and assign the results to two variables in one single line. The code below presents an example:

```
>>> A = 4
>>> X = 5
>>> Y = 9
>>> Z = 56
>>> B, C = A * X, Z + Y
>>> print (' A * X is:', B)
A * X is: 20
>>> print (' Z + Y is:', C)
Z + Y is: 65
```

In the following codes, we provide examples of applying some operators from the tables presented above.

```
>>> A = 4
>>> B = 20
```

Applying division:

```
>>> C= B // A
>>> print (' B divided by A is:', C)
B divided by A is: 5
```

Applying the modulus operator:

```
>>> C = B % A
>>> print (' The remainder of B divided by A is:', C)
The remainder of B divided by A is: 0
```

Operation on integers and float number:

>>> A, B = 2.4, 20
>>> C = B // 2.4
>>> print (' B divided by A is:', C)
B divided by A is: 8.0
>>> print (' The type of the results from an operation applied to an integer and float is:', type(C))
The type of the results from an operation applied to an integer and float is: <class 'float'>

As we can see from the example above, any operation applied to an integer and a float number always returns a float number type.

Python has several built-in mathematical functions available in the math module and comes within the standard library. These functions allow evaluating the trigonometric functions (i.e. cons, sin, tang...), the absolute value of a number, evaluating the integer part of a number, the power function, as well as rounding float number among others. The module math has also the number pi defined. In order to use these functions, the math module needs to be imported first.

In the following codes, we present examples of applying these functions. First, we import the math module:

```
>>> import math
```

Remember, in order to use a function within a module, we need to type module.function_name. For example, for the math module, all functions are called math.function_name. The examples below illustrate how math functions are called.

Using the pi number of the math module:

```
>>> print (' The number pi is:', math.pi)
The number pi is: 3.141592653589793
```

Calling the trigonometric functions from the math module:

```
>>> alpha = math.cos (math.pi)
>>> print (' The cos of pi is:', alpha)
The cos of pi is: -1.0
>>> alpha = math.sin (1)
>>> print (' The sin of 1 is:', alpha)
The sin of 1 is: 0.8414709848078965
>>> alpha = math.tan (1)
>>> print (' The tan of 1 is:', alpha)
The tan of 1 is: 1.5574077246549023
```

Applying the power function is the same as using the operator **:

```
>>> print (' 3 ** 2 is:', C)
3 ** 2 is: 9
>>> C = math.pow (3, 2)
>>> print (' 3 power 2 with pow function is:', C)
3 power 2 with pow function is: 9.0
```

Note that the operator ** returns an integer when the two numbers are integers whereas the math.pow() function always returns a float number. Functions presented in the following examples are from the standard library of Python and not included in the math module.

Evaluating the absolute value of a number:

```
>>> A, B = abs (-4), abs (6)
>>> print (' The absolute value of -4 and 6 are:', A, 'and', B)
The absolute value of -4 and 6 are: 4 and 6
```

Evaluating the integer part of a float number:

```
>>> A = int (6.7)
>>> print ('The integer part of 6.7 is:', A)
The integer part of 6.7 is: 6
```

Rounding the value of a float number:

>>> A = round (4.5)
>>> print (' The value of rounding 4.5 is:', A)
The value of rounding 4.5 is: 4

String Data Object in Python

Strings in Python are a sequence of characters stored in a list. Unlike other languages like C, for instance, Python does not support a char data object which a character singleton. In Python, a character singleton is basically a string of a single character. Strings in Python are immutable. In other words, once you define a string variable its size is fixed and cannot be changed after. As we mentioned before, a string is a sequence of characters stored in a list which means that string characters are saved in an orderly fashion from left to right. Each character in a string can be accessed by position because it is stored in a list.

To declare a variable a string, both single and double quotes can be used. Triple quotes are used when a variable is defined as a block of strings that extends over a few lines. The codes below illustrate examples of declaring variables using single, double and triple quotes.

```
>>> Ex1 = ' This is a string defined in a single quote'
>>> print (Ex1)
This is a string defined in a single quote
>>> Ex2 = " This is a string defined in a double quote"
>>> print (Ex2)
This is a string defined in a double quote
>>> Ex3 = """ This is an example of a string
... that extends on
... three lines """
>>> print (Ex3)
 This is an example of a string
that extends on
three lines
```

In fact, using a single or a double quote does not make any difference. Strings defined using a single or double quote are the same. For instance, we create the same string using both methods, Python will return the same exact result as in the example below:

```
>>> ' My string ', " My string "
(' My string ', ' My string ')
```

Python supports several built-in functions that handle strings, unlike other languages. These functions allow concatenation of two strings, repeating the same string, find a sequence of characters in a string, replace a sequence of characters of a string, and splitting a string. The following codes present these functions and illustrate with examples of how they can be used.

To concatenate two strings the operator ' + ' can be used. This operator concatenate strings of any length. For instance, we will concatenate the following strings:

```
>>> A = ' This is the first element of the concatenation example'
>>> B = ' This is the second element of the concatenation example'
>>> C = ' and this is the third element'
>>> X = A + B + C
>>> print (' The result of concatenation with the operator + is: \n', X)
The result of concatenation with the operator + is:
This is the first element of the concatenation example This is the second element of the concatenation example and this is the third element
```

A sequence of a string can be repeated n times using the operator ' * '. For instance:

>>> A = ' This is an example of repeating a sequence of string'
>>> B = A * 2
>>> print (' The string A repeated 2 times is:\n ', B)
The string A repeated 2 times is:
This is an example of repeating a sequence of string This is an example of repeating a sequence of string

To find a character or a sequence of characters within a string, Python has the function find(). This function is a method of the String class object that takes as input a character or a sequence of characters and returns the index of the first character of the sequence in the string. This method is used as in the example below:

>>> A = ' This is an example of the find function'
>>> A.find ('example ')
11

Remember that a string is a list and items of a string or its characters can be accessed by position. So, for the above example, the position returned by the find function is the position of the first character that was passed as an argument which is in this case ' e '. Therefore, if we try to get the 11th element of the string ' A ' we defined, we get the following output:

>>> A [11]
'e'

A sequence of characters in a string can be replaced using the function replace(). This function is also a method of the String class in Python like the find function and is called in the same manner. The replace function takes two arguments where the first argument is the sequence of characters to be replaced and the second argument is the sequence of characters to be replaced with. Let's see an example:

>>> A = ' This is an example of using the replace method'
>>> A.replace ('method', 'function')
' This is an example of using the replace function'

In the example above, we replaced ' method ' by ' function ' in the string variable ' A '.

To split a string into several strings, the split function is used. Like the previous methods, the split function is a method of the String class and is used in the same manner. The split function basically split a string according to the spaces in the string. The output is a list of strings where each item is a sequence of characters that forms the strings according to the spaces. The example below illustrates how this function works:

>>> A = ' This is an example of the split function'
>>> C = A. split()
>>> print (' The output of the split function is:\n', C)
The output of the split function is:
['This', 'is', 'an', 'example', 'of', 'the', 'split', 'function']

To evaluate the length of a string, the function len is used. This function takes as an argument a variable and it returns its length. In the code below, we illustrate how this function is applied:

```
>>> A = ' This is an example of the len function'
>>> L = len (A)
>>> print ('The length of the string variable A is:', L)
The length of the string variable A is: 38
```

List data object in Python

List data objects are a flexible heterogeneous data object that can contain items of different types. In addition, lists can expand, shrink, and change upon request. A list can be formed by any other data object including lists. Data is typically saved in lists in an orderly manner from left to right. Because items in lists are ordered, they can be accessed by indexing or position. We can perform slicing and indexing and concatenation. Lists in Python are mutable which means their size can be modified after they are defined. This means that we can delete items from a list or add new items to the list by index assignment. Python offers all basic functions to manipulate lists that include concatenation, sorting items in a list, deleting an element from a list, evaluating the length of a list, extending a list, reversing elements of a list, adding an element to a list, or repeating a list n times. The following examples illustrate how to apply these functions and to handle lists in Python.

Lists are defined in Python using brackets. This means that in order to define a list, items to be saved in the list should be written between brackets. For instance:

>>> A = [100, 40, 50]
>>> print (' My first list in Python is:', A)
My first list in Python is: [100, 40, 50]

Sometimes, it is useful to create an empty list in which we save items as we process information within a loop. We can create an empty list like in the example below:

>>> A = []
>>> print (' My first empty list in Python:', A)
My first empty list in Python: []

Items of a list can be extracted or accessed by their positions. In Python, indexing starts by 0 meaning that the position of the first element is 0. For example:

```
>>> A = [100, 40, 50]
>>> print (' The first item in my first list is:', A [0])
The first item in my first list is: 100
```

Python supports slicing to extract or modify items in a list. Note that an item can also be modified by its position. Slicing is typically used when we want to extract multiple elements at the same time. The examples below illustrate, in more detail, slicing.

```
>>> A = [100, 90, 600, 40, 500]
>>> print (' The first two elements of the list A are:', A [0:2])
The first two elements of the list A are: [100, 90]
>>> print (' The prior to the last element of the list A is:', A [-2])
The prior to the last two elements of the list A is: 40
>>> print (' The last two elements of the list A are:', A [-2:])
The last two elements of the list A are: [40, 500]
>>> print (' The three first elements of the list A are:', A [:3])
The three first elements of the list A are: [100, 90, 600]
```

As you can notice from the examples above, the last index of the slicing is not returned. It only indicates to Python where it should stop the slicing and the actual item corresponding to that index is not returned.

The following example is an illustration of the changing values of a list using slicing.

>>> A = [100, 90, 600, 40, 500]
>>> A [2:3] = [0,0]
>>> print (' The list after slicing assignment is:', A)
The list after slicing assignment is: [100, 90, 0, 0, 0, 40, 500]

When using slicing assignment, the number of new items should be the same as the number of items being replaced. Like in the example above, although we are assigning the same value (i.e. 0), we should assign a list of two items to change the value of the two items. If we try to assign a single value in this case, Python will throw an error like follows:

>>> A [2:3] = 0
Traceback (most recent call last):
 File "<stdin>", line 1, in <module>
TypeError: can only assign an iterable

To concatenate two lists, the operator ' + ' is used like for string data object. Concatenation conserves the same order in the lists passed as argument. For example:

>>> A = [100, 90, 600, 40, 500]
>>> B = [900, 34, 89, 789, 57]
>>> C = A + B
>>> print (' The concatenated lists is:', C)
The concatenated list is: [100, 90, 600, 40, 500, 900, 34, 89, 789, 57]

Like strings, a list can be repeated n times using the operator ' * '. For example:

>>> A = [100, 90, 600, 40, 500]
>>> C = A * 2
>>> print (' My list repeated 2 times is:', C)
My list repeated 2 times is: [100, 90, 600, 40, 500, 100, 90, 600, 40, 500]

The length of a list can be evaluated by the basic function of Python the len function. This function returns the number of elements saved in a list.

>>> A = [100, 90, 600, 40, 500]
>>> print (' The length of the list A is:', len (A))
The length of the list A is: 5

To sort elements of a list, the sort function is used. This function is a method specific to the list class object. In the example below, we present how this method is used.

>>> A = [100, 90, 600, 40, 500]
>>> A.sort()
>>> print (' This is an example of sorting a list and the result is: \n', A)
This is an example of sorting a list and the result is:
[40, 90, 100, 500, 600]

The sort function sort items of a list in ascending order. To reverse the items of the list, the method reverse is used.

This method is specific to the list class object and is as the sort function. Now, we can get the list sorted in a descending manner by applying both sorts and reverse like follows:

```
>>> A = [100, 90, 600, 40, 500]
>>> A.sort()
>>> A.reverse()
>>> print (' The reserved or sorted list A in descending order is: \n', A)
The reserved or sorted list A in descending order is:
 [600, 500, 100, 90, 40]
```

To add an item to a list, the append function is used. The append function is different than concatenation in the sense that appends is a method specific to list class object and take as input value while concatenation process two lists. They yield the same results in different ways. The append function is useful when you are processing data in a script and updating a list by adding each new item when available. The append function is called like the sort and reverse methods as follows:

```
>>> A = [100, 90, 600, 40, 500]
>>> A.append(10000)
>>> print (' This is an example of the append function and the result is: \n', A)
This is an example of the append function and the result is:
 [100, 90, 600, 40, 500, 10000]
```

Another function specific to the list class object is extended. This function allows also to add new items to a list. Unlike the append method, extend takes as in input argument a list. The following example illustrates how to add new items with the extend method.

```
>>> A = [100, 90, 600, 40, 500]
>>> A.extend([400, 900, 60])
>>> print ('This is an example of adding items with extend function: \n', A)
This is an example of adding items with extend function:
 [100, 90, 600, 40, 500, 400, 900, 60]
```

In Python two functions allow deleting items from a list which are pop and del functions. The first one, the pop function, deletes and returns the last item of a list.

This function is a specific method for the list class object. The second function, the del function, is more general and allows deleting any item or any number of items from a list by position. In the next examples, we illustrate how to use these two functions.

>>> A = [100, 90, 600, 40, 500, 400, 900, 60]
>>> A.pop()
60
>>> print (' This is an example of deleting with pop function: \n', A)
This is an example of deleting with pop function:
[100, 90, 600, 40, 500, 400, 900]
>>> del A [2:]
>>> print (' This is an example of deleting items with del function: \n', A)
This is an example of deleting items with del function:
[100, 90]

In the example, we deleted all elements from the second item of the list using slicing.

Dictionary data object in Python

The dictionary data object is another flexible data object supported in Python. Dictionaries are heterogeneous data object that enables saving data of different types including another dictionary. Dictionaries and lists both have some similarities in the context that they are both flexible and can shrink and extend upon request. The main difference between lists and dictionaries is that the way items are saved in these data objects and how they can be fetched. If items in lists are ordered and can be accessed by position, in dictionaries, items are not ordered and are accessed by key. Because dictionaries are a built-in object of Python, they support many data structures that you perhaps can need in developing an application and would have to define manually when working with low-level programming languages. In the same context, they also support several searching algorithms that would need to develop in low-level languages like C for instance. Indeed, using the indexing for dictionaries allows a fast search task. Dictionaries can be used as records or symbols for tables for other languages, or a representation of data structures that are sparse.

The main characteristics of dictionaries are as follows. Items of a dictionary are accessed by keys. In fact, items in a dictionary are associated with a key. In other words, a key is assigned for each set of values. When fetching a dataset, keys are used to extract the data that are saved in a particular key. Indexing operations can also be used to extract items out of a dictionary, however, the index is in the form of a key not a relative position within the dictionary. Items are unordered in a dictionary. Unlike lists, items in a dictionary do not follow a particular order. Python saves items in a dictionary in a random way which allows a fast lookup. The keys that are assigned for each set of data does not provide a physical position but a symbolic position of an item within a dictionary.

The length of a dictionary is variable meaning that it can expand or shrink without creating a new copy of the dictionary in question. They are heterogeneous in the sense that they can save in other types of data including lists or another dictionary. Items of a dictionary can be modified in place using index assignment. However, they do not allow the operations in sequences like strings or lists.

Items in dictionaries do not follow any order. Therefore, all operations that are based on a fixed order such as slicing or concatenation are not permitted and do not make any sense when working with dictionaries. However, dictionaries are the single data structure within Python that supports a representation of the category of mapping type meaning that objects can be mapped with keys to values. Finally, dictionaries can be considered as unordered tables. In fact, Python implements dictionaries as hash tables that can start with a small size, then expand if needed. Python uses algorithms that are optimized in order to find keys that make extracting items very fast.

Dictionaries in Python are defined by a set of keys for which a set of values are assigned and separated by a comma and enclosed between curly braces. Like lists, Python has several built-in functions that allow handling dictionaries that we are going to cover in the following code examples. The following table summarizes the operations that can be performed on dictionaries.

Table 4: List of operations to be performed on the dictionary data object.

Operator	Explanation
Dic = {}	Declaring an empty dictionary
Dic = {'age':10, 'name': 'john'}	Declaring a dictionary of two items
Dic ['age']	Indexing a dictionary by key
Dic.has_key ('age')	Test of membership
age' in Dic	Test of membership
Dic.keys ()	Get a list of keys
Dic.values ()	Get list of values
Dic.copy ()	Copies items of dictionary
Dic.get (key, default)	Get items
Len (Dic)	Get length of the dictionary
Dic [key] = value	Modifying or adding a value
Del Dic [key]	Deleting items

In the table above, we have an example of defining an empty dictionary and a dictionary of two items. We can also create a dictionary from other dictionaries. To get a sense of how to do so and how to use the functions in the table above, let's practice with some examples in the interactive session of Python.

To create an empty dictionary, we pass empty curly braces:

>>> Dic = {}
>>> print (' This is an example of an empty dictionary:', Dic)
This is an example of an empty dictionary: {}

To define a dictionary of items, values are assigned to keys. The following codes present an example:

>>> Dic = {'Name': 'John', 'Age': 100}
>>> print (' This is an example of an empty dictionary:', Dic)
This is an example of an empty dictionary: {'Name': 'John', 'Age': 100}

In the following example, we will see how we can define a dictionary that contains a dictionary.

>>> Dic = {' Pers': {' Name': 'John', 'Age': 10}}
>>> print (' This is an example of nested dictionary:', Dic)
This is an example of nested dictionary: {'Pers': {'Name': 'John', 'Age': 10}}

A dictionary can be also defined from lists. In the previous examples, each key is associated with single values. In the following examples, we illustrate how we can define a dictionary where each key is associated with a list of values.

>>> LL = ['John', 'Mike', 'Dave']
>>> Ag = [20, 30, 40]
>>> Dic = {'Name': LL, 'Age': Ag}
>>> print (' This is an example of a dictionary defined from lists:', dic)
This is an example of a dictionary defined from lists: {'Name': ['John', 'Mike', 'Dave'], 'Age': [20, 30, 40]}

To extract items from a dictionary, we use the same syntax of position indexing used for lists. The difference is we use keys instead of position. Let's see some real examples of how to extract items from a dictionary.

```
>>> LL = ['John', 'Mike', 'Dave']
>>> Ag = [20, 30, 40]
>>> dic = {'Name': LL, 'Age': Ag}
>>> print (' This is an example of extracting an item from a dictionary: \n', dic ['Name'])
 This is an example of extracting an item from a dictionary:
 ['John', 'Mike', 'Dave']
```

To extract keys of a dictionary, the keys method is used as follows:

```
>>> LL = ['John', 'Mike', 'Dave']
>>> Ag = [20, 30, 40]
>>> dic = {'Name': LL, 'Age': Ag}
>>> print (' This is an example of extracting keys of dictionary, keys are: \n', dic.keys())
 This is an example of extracting keys of dictionary, keys are:
 dict_keys (['Name', 'Age'])
```

We can verify if a key is part of a dictionary by using the logical in. The following presents an illustration of verifying the existence of a key in a dictionary.

>>> LL = ['John', 'Mike', 'Dave']
>>> Ag = [20, 30, 40]
>>> dic = {'Name': LL, 'Age': Ag}
>>> print ('This is an example of verifying if a key (here Age) is in dictionary:', 'Age' in dic)
This is an example of verifying if a key (here Age) is in dictionary:
True

The len function is a general function in Python that returns the length of a data object. It is applied to the dictionary the same as it is applied to lists and strings.

>>> LL = ['John', 'Mike', 'Dave']
>>> Ag = [20, 30, 40]
>>> dic = {'Name': LL, 'Age': Ag}
>>> print (' The length of the dictionary is:', len (dic))
The length of the dictionary is: 2

Values stored in a dictionary are extracted using the method values. This function is used as follows:

```
>>> LL = ['John', 'Mike', 'Dave']
>>> Ag = [20, 30, 40]
>>> dic = {'Name': LL, 'Age': Ag}
>>> print (' This is an example of extracting values of a dictionary:\n', dic.values ())
This is an example of extracting values of a dictionary:
 dict_values ([['John', 'Mike', 'Dave'], [20, 30, 40]])
```

Values stored in a dictionary can be replaced in place without creating a new dictionary. To do so, position indexing by key is used. The following code presents an example of changing values by key.

```
>>> LL = ['John', 'Mike', 'Dave']
>>> Ag = [20, 30, 40]
>>> dic = {'Name': LL, 'Age': Ag}
>>> print (' Dictionary before replacement:', dic)
Dictionary before replacement: {'Name': ['John', 'Mike', 'Dave'], 'Age': [20, 30, 40]}
>>> dic ['Name'] = ['Markus', 'David', 'Peter']
>>> print (' Dictionary after replacement:', dic)
Dictionary after replacement: {'Name': ['Markus', 'David', 'Peter'], 'Age': [20, 30, 40]}
```

Items from a dictionary can be deleted using position indexing and the del function. For instance,

>>> LL = ['John', 'Mike', 'Dave']
>>> Ag = [20, 30, 40]
>>> dic = {'Name': LL, 'Age': Ag}
>>> print (' Dictionary before deletion is:', dic)
Dictionary before deletion is: {'Name': ['Markus', 'David', 'Peter'], 'Age': [20, 30, 40]}
>>> del dic ['Age']
>>> print (' Dictionary after deletion is:', dic)
Dictionary after deletion is: {'Name': ['Markus', 'David', 'Peter']}

Items can be added to a dictionary using position indexing like in the following example:

>>> LL = ['John', 'Mike', 'Dave']
>>> dic = {'Name': LL}
>>> print (' Dictionary before adding new item is:', dic)
Dictionary before adding new item is: {'Name': ['Markus', 'David', 'Peter']}
>>> dic ['Age'] = [90, 30, 50]
>>> print (' Dictionary after adding new item is:', dic)
Dictionary after adding new item is: {'Name': ['Markus', 'David', 'Peter'], 'Age': [90, 30, 50]}

So far, we covered in this chapter all basic and flexible data objects supported by Python. In the next section, we will cover the last data object which is tuples. This data object is relatively simple to handle, and as you can see, you already learned basics functions that might be used on tuples too from reading these sections about the other data objects.

Tuples data object in Python

Tuples like dictionaries and lists are a collection of data of different types. Tuples are very similar to lists. However, tuples cannot be changed. Indeed, tuples are less flexible than lists and are immutable. Items of tuples are typically written between parenthesis instead of brackets like lists. Tuples have similar characteristics as lists. Items in tuples are ordered according to their positions. Items in a tuple can be accessed by their positions. Therefore, tuples support indexing, slicing, concatenation, repetition, and globally all operations performed on strings and lists. Tuples are similar to string in the context that both do not allow changing in size or items in place. Tuples cannot expand or shrink and their size is fixed once it is defined. The heterogeneous data object supports storing data of different types. In the following code examples, we illustrate how to perform some operations like indexing, concatenation, slicing, and others on tuples.

First, we illustrate some examples of defining a tuple.

```
>>> A = ()
>>> print (' This is an example of an empty tuple: ', A)
This is an example of an empty tuple: ()
>>> A = (1,)
>>> print (' This is an example of a one item tuple: ', A)
This is an example of a one item tuple: (1,)
>>> A = (1, 'John', 6.7, 90)
>>> print (' This is an example of a 4 items tuple: ', A)
This is an example of a 4 items tuple: (1, 'John', 6.7, 90)
>>> A = 1, 'John', 6.7, 90
>>> print (' This is another example of a 4 items tuple same as the one before: \n', A)
This is another example of a 4 items tuple same as the one before:
 (1, 'John', 6.7, 90)
>>> A = 1, 'John', (6.7, 90)
>>> print (' This is an example of a nested tuple: ', A)
This is an example of a nested tuple: (1, 'John', (6.7, 90))
```

Note from the examples above that if values assigned to a variable without brackets or parenthesis, Python will automatically consider the variable as a tuple. Although in the case of tuples, parenthesis is optional. In order to declare a variable as a tuple, it is a best practice to use parenthesis.

This also helps code readability. Note also that parenthesis in Python encloses an expression. So, if a tuple from a single item is to be declared, use the syntax presented in the examples above. If a single value is written between parenthesis, it will not consider it as tuple but rather just a value.

Tuples have no specific methods like lists. However, the basic Python operations performed on lists and strings apply to tuples as well.

To concatenate two tuples, the operator ' +' is used. For example:

```
>>> A = (1, 4, 60)
>>> B = (90, 50, 40)
>>> print (' This is an example of tuple concatenation: ', A + B)
This is an example of tuple concatenation: (1, 4, 60, 90, 50, 40)
```

To repeat a tuple n times, the operator ' *' is used as in the example below:

```
>>> A = (1, 4, 60)
>>> print (' This is an example of tuple repeated 2 times: ', A * 2)
This is an example of tuple repeated 2 times: (1, 4, 60, 1, 4, 60)
```

To extract an item from a tuple, we can use either indexing or slicing as illustrated in the examples below:

```
>>> A = (1, 4, 60)
>>> print (' This is an example of extracting an item from a tuple by indexing: ', A [1])
This is an example of extracting an item from a tuple by indexing: 4
>>> print ('This is an example of extracting an item from a tuple by slicing: ', A [:1])
This is an example of extracting an item from a tuple by slicing: (1,)
```

Note that when extracting items from a tuple, it returns a tuple even though it is a single value.

To sort items stored in a tuple, it should be converted to a list then sorted. Like mentioned before, tuples do not have specific methods like lists. The following example illustrates how to order a tuple:

```
>>> A = (100, 4, 60)
>>> print (' This is a tuple before sorting: ', A)
This is a tuple before sorting: (100, 4, 60)
>>> T = list (A)
>>> print (' This is a tuple converted to a list: ', list(A))
This is a tuple converted to a list: [100, 4, 60]
>>> T.sort ()
>>> print (' This is the list sorted', T)
This is the list sorted [4, 60, 100]
>>> A = tuple (T)
>>> print (' This is the tuple sorted: ', A)
This is the tuple sorted: (4, 60, 100)
```

Note that the function list() allows converting an item to a list and the tuple() function convert an object to a tuple. In fact, both functions list() and tuple() create new objects. Here, we just have overwritten the existing ones which makes it like a conversion of data types.

The immutability characteristics apply only to the tuple data object and not to items that it contains. For instance, if a tuple contains a list, the size of the list can be changed but not the tuple itself. Let's see an example to make it more comprehensible.

```
>>> A = (' Name', [20, 40, 50], 0)
>>> print (' This is an example of a tuple containing a list:', A)
This is an example of a tuple containing a list: ('Name', [20, 40, 50], 0)
>>> A [1][2] = 9000
>>> print ('This is an example of changing an item in a list within a tuple:', A)
This is an example of changing an item in a list within a tuple: ('Name', [20, 40, 9000], 0)
```

If we try to change an item from the tuple like follows, Python throws an error:

```
>>> A [1] = 'Age'
Traceback (most recent call last):
 File "<stdin>", line 1, in <module>
TypeError: 'tuple' object does not support item assignment
```

In this chapter, we covered all built-in data objects in Python which are number, strings, lists, dictionaries, and tuples. The last data object, tuples, are heterogeneous data object that allows storing data of different type like lists and dictionaries but is less flexible. You are probably wondering why to use tuples.

If they are not flexible, using lists instead would make more sense. Indeed, lists are more flexible, but they can be changed through your script. On the contrary, tuples cannot be changed or altered after they are defined. In addition, tuples may be of interest where lists cannot, for instance, as keys for dictionaries. Also, some functions in Python require variable in the form of tuples, not lists. As a general rule, lists are the go-to when the data need to be in ordered data structure and may be changed throughout the script. Otherwise, tuples are the best choice.

Chapter 4: Python Operators

In this chapter, we will cover the different statements in Python as well as the Boolean expressions and conditional statement which are the if tests and loops. Overall, we will cover the statements that allow processing data that are stored in the data object that we presented in the previous chapter. At the end of this chapter, you will acquire basic skills to develop and run some logic Python scripts.

Python Statements Syntax

Before diving into logic if test and loops and logic conditions, we are going to run over the basic syntax of Python. Statements are basically the expression you write that instruct what the Python interpreter should do. In other words, statements are instructions into your program. In the following table, we present a global statement that can be used in Python.

Table 5: List of Statements supported in Python.

Statement	Explanation	Illustration
Assignment	Create a variable	A, B = 90, 'Age'
print	Display objects	print (' This is an example')
call	Launching a function	stdout.write('Example\n')
while else	Global loop	while T: print ('Example')
for else	Iteration in a sequence	for i in list: print(i)
if/elif/else	Selection of tasks	if A in text: print ('Example if test')
break and continue	To jump into a specific task in loops	while T: if not A: break
try, except and finally	Exceptions catching	try: tasks / except: print ('Example Error')
raise	To trigger an exception	raise Endlocation
import	Module importing	import math
import from	Import from a module	from sys import stdout
def, return and yield	Defining functions	def fct(a): return a * 3

class	To build objects	class subclass: newData=[]
global	Defining a global variable	def fct(): global a, return a * 3
del	To delete items	del data
assert	To check to debug	assert A == B

Statements that are related to larger programming subjects like developing functions, modules, and debugging will be covered separately in the upcoming chapters of this book. Chapters are dedicated to each programming subject. In this chapter, we will cover the assignment syntax, expression statements, the if test, and the loops. Let's start with the basic statement which is the assignment.

So far, in this chapter, we have been already using the assignment statement. The assignment statement allows assigning a data object to a variable name. Basically, you write an assignment statement using the operator '=' where on the left, you have the target, and the on the right is that the data to be assigned.

The target can be either a variable name or component of an object. On the right can be a single value or an expression that evaluates an object. Overall, the assignment is very simple, but you should consider some properties. Assignment in Python saves objects references in names or data structure. When an assignment is used, it does not copy the object, but it creates a reference to the object.

Unlike C language, for example, variables in Python are similar to pointers and not just data storage. This means when you use or modify a variable inside a function, it is modified through the entire script not just locally. On the contrary, if a variable in C is modified in a function, it is modified only locally and not in the whole script. When first assigned, names are created. In Python, a variable name is created on the first time you assign a value to it. Python does not require a pre-declaration of variable names beforehand. When assigned, the variable name is replaced by the value that references in each expression they belong to. Before being referenced, the variable name must be assigned.

If a variable name is used before it is assigned to a reference data object, Python throws an error. Python uses some other implicit assignments when importing modules, defining functions or classes, in function arguments that we will see later in this book. Assignment works the same in any context and whether it is implicit or explicit, the assignment always binds an object reference to a variable name. Assignment has a few forms that are presented in the table below.

Table 6: Forms of Assignment Statements

Statement	Explanation
A = 5	Basic assignment form
A, B = 5, 6	Multiple assignment
A = 5, 6	Assignment of tuple
A = (5, 6)	Assignment of tuple
A = [4, 5]	Assignment of list
A = B = 'true'	Multiple target assignment

The first two forms of the assignment are the most basic forms. The three following forms of assignment (list and tuple assignment) are called list /tuple unpacking assignment.

In these forms of assignment, Python creates first a tuple /list of the elements on the right. Then it pairs from left to right to the variable name. The last form assignment, multiple target assignment, Python assigns the same data reference to multiple target variables. This assignment is the same as writing two lines of codes to assign A = 'true' and B = 'true'. In the following code examples, we will cover some illustration of assignment forms and tricks coding in Python.

Here we present some basic unpacking assignments.

```
>>> Age = 30
>>> Name = ' John'
>>> A, B = Age, Name
>>> print (' This is an example of tuple unpacking assignment: ')
>>> A, B
(30, ' John')
>>> [X, Y] = [Age, Name]
>>> print (' This is an example of list unpacking assignment: ', X, Y)
This is an example of list unpacking assignment: [30, ' John']
```

The reference values found on the right is stored in a temporary tuple. Since the temporary tuple is defined by Python, tuple unpacking assignment may be used to replace 2 variables while not having to define a temporary variable. The following example illustrates how to swap two variables with unpacking assignment.

```
>>> Age = 30
>>> Name = 'John'
>>> Age, Name
(30, 'John')
>>> Name, Age = Age, Name
>>> print ('This is an example of swapping variables with unpacking assignment: ')
This is an example of swapping variables with unpacking assignment:
>>> Age, Name
('John', 30)
```

In Python, any sequence of values or data can be assigned to a tuple or list on the condition that the sequence has the same length. A list of values can be assigned to a tuple and vice-versa. A string can also be assigned to a tuple.

In general, Python would assign the right items to the left items in sequence from left to right by position. Let's see some illustrations.

```
>>> [X, Y, Z] = (30, 400, 50)
>>> print (' This is an example of assigning a tuple to a list:')
This is an example of assigning a tuple to a list:
>>> X, Y, Z
(30, 400, 50)
>>> (X, Y, Z) = 'ade'
>>> print (' This is an example of assigning a string to a tuple:')
This is an example of assigning a string to a tuple:
>>> X, Y, Z
('a', 'd', 'e')
```

An unpacking assignment allows assigning a sequence of integer to multiple variables. In fact, Python has a built-in function which is a range that returns a sequence of integers. This function is very useful when working with for loops that we are going to see later in this chapter. In the next example, we provide an illustration of assigning a series of integers to a tuple.

```
>>> A, B, C = range (3)
>>> print (' This is an example assigning a sequence of integers:', A, B, C)
This is an example assigning a sequence of integers: 0 1 2
```

Now that we have covered the assignment statement, it is worth mentioning that rules should be respected when choosing a variable name. We have already seen in Chapter 2 of this book that variable names should always start by an underscore or a letter and only alpha-numeric characters are permitted. In general, a name of a variable should respect the following syntax: letter or underscore + letter, underscore or digit. A named variable like 1_var, var# or $%var is not permitted variable names. In Python, the case is important and variables names are case sensitive. For instance, Var, var, and VAR are three different variable names. Python has reversed words that are permitted to be variable names. Basically, these reversed words are lowercase and are used by the Python system. For instance, if you try assigning a value to 'and ' Python will throw a syntax error:

```
>>> and = 4
File "<stdin>", line 1
and = 4
    ^
SyntaxError: invalid syntax
```

The same variable name can be used if it is uppercase:

```
>>> AND = 4
>>> AND
4
```

Overall, the reversed words cannot be redefined. This applies also to module and function names. You might be able to define a module as ' and.py' or a function as ' and() ', but Python will generate an error when you try to call the function or import the module. The following table presents all reversed words that are not permitted as variable names.

Table 7: Reverse word in Python not permitted as variable names.

and	elif	global	or	yield
assert	else	if	pass	def
break	except	import	print	continue
class	exec	del	from	for
finally	in	is	return	try
lambda	while	not	raise	

In addition to the rules mentioned above to name a variable, there are some conventions that should be considered. They are a requirement but considered the common practice. The names of the variables that end and start with 2 underscores, for example, __X__, are typically considered by the interpreter of Python as system variable names. Naming variables in that manner should be avoided. The statement ' from module import ' cannot import names with a single underscore like _name. If a variable name starts with two underscores and does not end with another two, it is located to enclosing classes. A name that is only in the form of a single underscore (i.e. _) save the last expression result in the interactive session of Python.

These were the major naming rules and conventions that you should consider when choosing a name to a variable. In the following examples, we are going to cover some useful assignment statement that is commonly used within the if test and loops that we are going to cover later in this chapter. These assignment statements are inspired by the C programming language and mainly a shorthand. They typically combine an assignment with a binary expression. The following table summarizes these statements known as augmented assignment statements.

Table 8: List of Python augmented assignment.

Assignment	Equivalent	Assignment	Equivalent
A += B	A = A + B	A -= B	A = A - B
A &= B	A = A & B	A ** = Y	A = A ** B
A // = B	A = A // B	A /= B	A = A / B
A %= B	A = A % B	A | = B	A = A | B

Let's go back to the Python interactive session and see some examples of these assignments. We start first by the operator '+='.

```
>>> A = 10
>>> A = A + 1
>>> print (' A incremented by traditional assignment:', A)
A incremented by traditional assignment: 11
>>> A = 10
>>> A += 1
>>> print (' A incremented by augmented assignment:', A)
A incremented by augmented assignment: 11
```

Note that both yield to the very same results. However, the augmented assignment ' A += 1 ' is faster because Python needs to evaluate the variable 'A' one time. On the contrary with the basic form ' A = A + 1', the variable needs to be evaluated twice because it appears in the expression twice. This augmented assignment '+=' works as concatenation when applied to strings and, as mentioned, works faster than the basic concatenation formulation.

```
>>> A = 'Example'
>>> A += ' number 1'
>>> print (' This is an example of augmented assignment on strings type:', A)
This is an example of augmented assignment on strings type: Example number 1
```

The same augmented assignment can be applied to a list. For instance,

```
>>> List = [30, 40, 50]
>>> List += [2, 5, 8]
>>> print (' This is an example of augmented assignment on List type:', List)
This is an example of augmented assignment on List type: [30, 40, 50, 2, 5, 8]
```

In short, augmented assignment perform faster because variables on the left need to be evaluated once and require less typing. In addition, they allow the interpreter to choose automatically the best technique to evaluate the expression.

If an object supports in-place modification like lists, the augmented assignment would perform the in-place modification instead of creating a copy.

Syntax rules in Python

Before diving into if test and loops, in this section, we are going to address the syntax rules that should be followed when coding with Python. Python syntax is generally simple. However, there are some rules to respect. Globally, there are no braces or parentheses around the statements block in Python. Instead, Python relies on indentation to delimit or group blocks of code nested under a header. Unlike other programming languages, Python does not use a semicolon to indicate the end of the statement. The line end is the statement end on that particular line.

When launched, program statements are executed by Python from first to last until there is an indication to jump a block of statements. Python would jump a block of statements if it meets an if a test or a loop as we are going to see later in this chapter. These statements are called the control flow because they control which statements to run or to jump. Blank lines are generally ignored by the interpreter as well as lines starting by a ' # ' character. In fact, any line that starts with the ' # ' character is considered a comment.

Hence, it is ignored by the Python interpreter. There is another type of comments supported by Python that is known as the documentation strings. They are also known as docstrings in short. This form of comment is retained by the Python interpreter. They show up at the header of a program file. They are associated with objects and can also be printed alongside the documentation. Although Python interpreter retains the docstrings, they are ignored.

Remember that indentation is very important in Python and indicates the level of a block. If the indentation is not used appropriately and consistently, Python throws an error. The if statements and loops generally have a header line as we are going to see in the following chapters. Block of codes to run each header whether it is a loop or an if test. Globally, when developing a Python program, the form or syntax of the program should look like:

```
Code block level 0
Header statement:
        Code block level 1
        Header statement:
                Code block level 2
                ....
        Code block level 1
Code block level 0
```

Note that in the example syntax presented above, each code block line up to the right in the same distance as considered from the same block. Codes that are deeply nested are just more intended to the right compared to the upper enclosing code.

If a statement doesn't fit in a single line because it is too long, there are few rules to respect to make them continue on a few lines. Python support continuing a statement in more than one line if it is enclosed between brackets, parenthesis, or curly braces. All statements that are between parenthesis, assigning lists, dictionaries, and tuples can be performed on more than one line. These statements end at the line where the closing part appears.

Only the first line where the statement begins should be intended correctly and the continuous lines can be at any level. For instance, we declare in the following example a list on several lines:

```
>>> A = [ 9,
... 8,
... 10,
... 100]
>>> print (' That was a list declaration on multiple lines:', A)
That was a list declaration on multiple lines: [9, 8, 10, 100]
```

This type of statements continuing on several lines can be used for anything between () like expressions, or function headers or arguments. For example:

```
>>> A = 2
>>> B = 3
>>> if (A == 1
... and B == 3):
... print ('YES')
... else:
... print('NO')
...
NO
```

Note that in this example, only the statement under the header of the if and else statements should be intended. The continuing line of the if the header does not have to be intended.

Python support writing more than one statement in one line separated by a semicolon. For instance:

>>> A = 3; B = 90; C = 900
>>> print (' That was an example of multiple statements in a single line:', A, B, C)
That was an example of multiple statements in a single line: 3 90 900

Python If Test and Its Variations

This chapter section will cover the if test which is a statement that allows choosing from a series of possible operations according to the result of a test. In this, we will cover also the Boolean expressions and truth tests. We will also see in detail the embedded statement syntax.

The if statement is typically a formal procedure in programming languages. This statement is in the form of if test then a set of options of operations to perform or another elif (i.e. else if) and ends with a block of else. The block of else is optional. After every test (if and elif) and else, there is an embedded block of operations that is indented under the test header. When running Python on if test, it performs the block of operations that are assigned to the first test which is satisfied (i.e. returns true) otherwise, it performs the else block if all tests are not true. Basically, the if statement takes the general form presented below:

```
if < condition or test >:
        < block of statements >
elif < condition or test >:
        < block of statements >
else:
        < block of statements >
```

Only the if statement and the associated block are required. The other elif and else blocks are optional. Let's practice some examples in the interactive session and see how the if statement how works under Python.

In the very basic case, an if statement can be run alone when you need to run an operation when a condition is met. The following code example provides an illustration.

```
>>> X = 9
>>> if (X == 9):
... print (' YES ')
...
YES
```

Notice here that the prompt changed to ' ... ' which means the continuation of lines in the basic Operating system. If working in IDLE, you have to intend the block after the If header. Here in the interactive session, a blank line ends the statement and runs the if block. In the following code, we illustrate the most common form used of the if test:

```
>>> X = 0
>>> if (X == 9):
... print (' YES ')
... else:
... print (' NO ')
...
NO
```

In the next code example, we provide an illustration of the complete form of the if statement with all blocks. This is typically used when you have multiple conditions to evaluate in order to choose to right operations to perform within your code.

```
>>> A = ' TIGER '
>>> if (A == 'John '):
... print ('HOW are you, John?')
... elif (A == 'Dog'):
... print (' What is the name of the dog? ')
... else:
... print (' WARNING: DANGER ')
...
WARNING: DANGER
```

Note that, in this example, Python runs through all blocks because they all return false statement. Now, you might be wondering how to select an action based on the value of a variable. In fact, Python does not have a switch or case statements like C programming language or Pascal. If you are not familiar with these programming languages, the switch and case are statements that allow performing an action according to its value. In Python, the if/elif/else statement is used in series instead. In the following example, we provide an illustration of performing an operation based on the value of the variable ' A '.

```
>>> A = 3
>>> if (A == 1):
... print (' The month is January')
... elif (A == 2):
... print (' The month is February')
... elif (A == 3):
... print (' The month is March')
... else:
... print (' This is another month')
...
The month is March
```

Another way to implement this example and requires less typing is by using a dictionary. In fact, a dictionary associates with each key value. To use a dictionary in the previous example, we should do something like:

```
>>> B = {'1': ' The month is January ', ' 2 ': ' The month is February ',
...      '3': ' The month is March '}
>>> print (B.get (' 1 '))
This month is January
>>> print (B.get (5))
None
```

Note here that when a key is not found in the dictionary, it returns None by default which would be like the else statement in an if test. In short, dictionaries can be a very good alternative to implement a simple procedure that selects an option according to variable possible values where these possible values are the keys of the dictionary.

In the rest of this section, we are going to discuss the truth test that is usually used within an if test. In the previous chapters, we have introduced comparisons operator used on strings and numbers and so on. Basically, these are Boolean operators that return True or False, 0 or 1 depending on the operation or the comparison used. Overall, true is returned when an object is a non-zero number or not empty. False is returned if an object is zero number or empty or is None. The equality test and comparisons are applied to data objects and return 1 or 0. The logic operators 'and' and 'or' returns true or false. Let's see some examples in the Python interactive session.

```
>>> A = 3
>>> B = 5
>>> A == 3 and B == 4
False
>>> A == 3 or B == 4
True
>>> [] or 5
5
```

Note here that in the last line, Python evaluates both the left and the right side and returns the right value or because the left is false. Basically, when used in an if test or a while loop, Python uses a Boolean which is a logical true or false.

Loops in Python (while and for loop)

In this section, we discuss the main two loops in Python that repeats a block of code over and over. The first loop format is the while loop which supports a general looping statement and the second loop format is the for loop that goes through elements of a sequence data structure and runs a specific code. Other forms of loops are supported in Python that includes 'break' and 'continue' which we will cover in the next section.

A while loop is a broad form of iteration construct. The while loop typically runs the same code over and over as long as a condition is true. When this is evaluated to false, Python interpreter skips the code intended under the while header and runs the following code statements. In the simplest form of the while loop, the syntax is as follows:

> while < test or condition >:
>   Block of code

Python will run, in this case, the block of code until the test is evaluated to false. The other form of Python is more complex looks like:

```
while < test or condition >:
        Block of code
else:
        Block of code 2
```

In this form, Python will run the block of code 2 if it does not exit the while loop with a break. Now, let's go back to the interactive session of Python and see some examples of a while loop.

```
>>> A = ' NAME '
>>> while A:
... print (' This is an example of while loop:', A)
... A = A [1:]
...
This is an example of while loop: NAME
This is an example of while loop: AME
This is an example of while loop: ME
This is an example of while loop: E
```

In this example, the while loop runs the code as long as the variable 'A ' is not empty. The code consists of printing the value of the variable 'A' and removing one character. Note that one major problem that you should pay attention to when using the while loop is that this loop may run forever if the test is always evaluated as true. Hence, checking and making sure that the test is evaluated to false at some point to exit the loop.

The for loop consist of iterating through elements of a sequence object that can be string, list, dictionary, tuple or any other class object. Basically, the number of iterations is known beforehand unlike the while loop that runs according to a test value. The for loop syntax is very easy and takes the form of a header line and block of statements to run over and over and optionally an else statement like the while loop. The header of the for loop indicates a target and the data object that it iterates trough. The general syntax is as follows:

```
for < i > in < data object >:
    block of code
else:
    block of code 2
```

When running a for loop, Python attribute elements of the data object to the 'i' variable. Then it evaluates the block of the code for each item of the data object stored in 'i'. This variable 'i' is assigned in the header of the loop and can be changed inside the loop and is updated automatically to the next element in the sequence whenever the control is evaluating the header of the loop. Typically, this variable takes the value of the last item evaluated in the sequence when the loop is over. If the loop did not exit with a break statement and was run accurately, the variable 'i' would refer to the very last item in the sequence. The optional else block works similarly as for the while loop. If the for loop did not exit with a break, it will run the code block assigned to the else statement.

Now, let's see examples in the interactive session of Python. The first example presents an illustration of applying a for loop on a list of strings. This example goes through string items of a list and prints each element.

```
>>> List = ['John', 'Brian', 'Mike', 'James']
>>> for i in List:
... print ('Name is:', i)
...
Name is: John
Name is: Brian
Name is: Mike
Name is: James
```

Note here that in the loop, each string element is assigned to the variable 'i'. We can also use the position indexing to loop over items of a list. For the previous example, we would do:

```
>>> List = ['John', 'Brian', 'Mike', 'James']
>>> for i in range (len (List)):
... print ('Name is:', List [i])
...
Name is: John
Name is: Brian
Name is: Mike
Name is: James
```

The second application of the for loop is useful when you are assigning elements from the sequence to another sequence by position. We will see in the next example an application of the for loop on a list of numbers. In this example, we compute the sum of elements of a list.

```
>>> A = [10, 200, 4, -100]
>>> X = 0
>>> for i in A:
...     X+= i
...     print (' A loop example on list of numbers, the sum is:', X)
...
A loop example on list of numbers, the sum is: 10
A loop example on list of numbers, the sum is: 210
A loop example on list of numbers, the sum is: 214
A loop example on list of numbers, the sum is: 114
```

If a single statement is to be evaluated within the loop body, the for loop header and the statement can be written in the same line. For instance, the previous example becomes without the print statement as:

```
>>> A = [10, 200, 4, -100]
>>> X = 0
>>> for i in A: X+=i
...
>>> print (' This is an example of for loop in a single statement, the sum is:', X)
This is an example of for loop in a single statement, the sum is: 114
```

The for loop works the same on a sequence of tuples where the target value will be assigned a tuple. The following two examples illustrate how the for loop work on a tuple sequence.

```
>>> T = ('John', 'Mike', ' Samuel')
>>> for i in T:
... print ('Name in the tuple is:', i)
...
Name in the tuple is: John
Name in the tuple is: Mike
Name in the tuple is: Samuel
```

If a list of tuples is provided the loop for works the same. For instance:

>>> T = [('John', 30), ('Mike', 40), ('Samuel', 40)]
>>> for i in T:
... print ('Name and age in list of tuples is:', i)
...
Name and age in list of tuples is: ('John', 30)
Name and age in list of tuples is: ('Mike', 40)
Name and age in list of tuples is: ('Samuel', 40)

In the above example, at each iteration, the target variable ' i ' is assigned a tuple that is in the list sequence. Another way to use the loop for, in this case, is to iterate through two-variable targets where each variable is assigned an element of the tuple in the list. We can apply this to the previous example as follows:

>>> T = [('John', 30), ('Mike', 40), ('Samuel', 40)]
>>> for (i, j) in T:
... print (' Name in the list tuple is', i, 'Age in the list tuple is', j)
...
Name in the list tuple is John Age in the list tuple is 30
Name in the list tuple is Mike Age in the list tuple is 40
Name in the list tuple is Samuel Age in the list tuple is 40

A function that is useful when working with loops, in particular, the for loop is the range function. This function basically takes as an input of one or two arguments. Then it generates a sequence of order values according to the value of the input arguments. If only one argument is supplied as input, then it generates values in the range 0 to the input value. If it is supplied with two input arguments, then it generates values from the first input value to the second input value. The following code presents an illustration of the range function supplied with one and two arguments.

```
>>> for i in range (4):
... print ('Example of range with one input argument here 4, values are:', i)
...
Example of range with one input argument here 4, values are: 0
Example of range with one input argument here 4, values are: 1
Example of range with one input argument here 4, values are: 2
Example of range with one input argument here 4, values are: 3
>>> for i in range (3, 6):
... print ('Example of range with 2 input arguments here 3 & 6, values are:', i)
...
Example of range with 2 input arguments here 3 & 6, values are: 3
Example of range with 2 input arguments here 3 & 6, values are: 4
Example of range with 2 input arguments here 3 & 6, values are: 5
```

We can pass optionally the third argument to the range function. When supplied, this argument is used as a step to generate values from the first to the second input argument values. The next example provides an illustration of the range function supplied with three input arguments.

>>> for i in range (3, 10, 2):
... print ('Example of range with 3 input arguments here 3 & 10 & 2, values are:', i)
...
Example of range with 3 input arguments here 3 & 10 & 2, values are: 3
Example of range with 3 input arguments here 3 & 10 & 2, values are: 5
Example of range with 3 input arguments here 3 & 10 & 2, values are: 7
Example of range with 3 input arguments here 3 & 10 & 2, values are: 9

Notice that whether it is supplied by one or two input arguments, the range function does not include this input value in the returned range values. As you can see from these examples, the range function is very useful with loops to repeat a sequence of operations over and over for a specific number of times.

The while loop and the for loop can have a much-complicated syntax that allows jumping or exiting the loop when a specific condition is met or a test that evaluates to true. In general, loops can be associated with the statement's break and continue. In the next section, we cover the usage of break and continue within loops of Python.

Continue, Break and Pass Statements with Python Loops

Now that you have seen Python loops, while and for, we will cover the two statements continue and break. These statements only work within a loop. We will also see in more detail the else statement which is related to the break statement.

The break statement allows jumping all the codes enclosed in the closest loop. In other words, it exits the enclosing loop. The continue statement, on the other hand, jumps to the closest enclosing loop header. The pass statement is equivalent to not doing anything which is basically a placeholder of an empty statement. The pass statement is typically used when there is no required action to take and works as an empty body for a statement that is compounded. Given these definitions, the general complex format of the while loop is as follows:

```
while < test or condition >:
        Block of code
        if <test 1 or condition 1>: break
        if <test or condition 2>: continue

    else:
        Block of code 2
```

Note that the break and continue can be placed anywhere within the body loop. However, they are typically placed within an if test to operate as a response to the returned value of a test or a condition as presented above. Now, let's go back to an interactive session to see some examples.

In this first example, we will see how the continue statement allows jumping nested statements. The illustration presented displays all odd numbers inferior to 10 and jumps even numbers.

```
>>> A = 10
>>> while A:
...     A = A - 1
...     if ((A % 2) == 0): continue
...     print(A)
...
9
7
5
3
1
```

In this example, there is no need to enclose the print statement within an if test because the continue statement will skip it if the test ' (A % 2) == 0 ' is evaluated to true. Hence, the print statement is run only if the continue statement is not run. The continue statement used here is similar to a 'goto' in other programming languages. If you are just starting with

Python, it is best to use continue sparingly. The above example can be written in a more readable way with the print statement assigned to an if test as follows:

```
>>> A = 10
>>> while A:
... A = A - 1
... if (A % 2 != 0) :
... print(A)
...
9
7
5
3
1
```

The next example provides an illustration of the while loop with a break statement. In this example, we read input data from the user until he writes an end.

```
>>> name= []
>>> while name != 'end':
...         name = input ('Enter a name, to stop enter end: ')
...
Enter a name, to stop enter end: 'John'
Enter a name, to stop enter end: 'Mike'
Enter a name, to stop enter end: 'Liam'
Enter a name, to stop enter end: 4
Enter a name, to stop enter end: end
>>>
```

The function input() here is a function of Python version 3 that reads input from the keyboard. Note that when the loop keeps reading from the standard input until the end is entered. Then Python returned >>> into the prompt which means it is ready to take other statements.

In the following example, we illustrate how to combine the break and the else statements in a while loop. In this example, we determine if a given number is prime or not by looking for the numbers factors which are superior to 1.

```
>>> A = 7
>>> B = A / 2
>>> while B > 1:
... if (B % A == 0):
... print (A, ' is factor of', B)
... break
... B = B - 1
... else:
... print (' The number', B, 'is prime')
...
The number 0.5 is prime
```

The break here is very useful that works as a flag when exiting the while loop. In this example, instead of adding an if test to evaluate the value after the while loop is over, a break is inserted to exit when a factor is found. Otherwise, if the break is not met, the loop assumes that a number is a prime number.

Note that even if the loop does not run at all in case the header is false, to begin with, it will return or run the statement assigned to the else because it did not exit with a break in this case. If we try that on the previous example (i.e. B == 0), we still get the message 'The number is prime'.

```
>>> B = 0
>>> while B > 1:
... if (B % A == 0):
... print (A, ' is factor of', B)
... break
... B = B - 1
... else:
... print (' The number', B, 'is prime')
...
The number 0 is prime
```

The else might seem a bit confusing because it is specific to Python's programming. You can think of the else as a way of coding some flags that catch the exit of a loop without explicitly hard coding test to check those flags.

Let's say that you are coding a loop that search for an item in a sequence of values and you want to know, after the loop is over, whether it was found or not. You might think of coding something that looks like the following code:

```
>>>A = [20, 200, 2, 90]
>>>inList = 'NO'
>>>i = 0
>>> while (i < len (A) and inList == 'NO'):
...         if (A [i] == 0):
...                 inList = 'YES'
...         else:
...                 i = i+1
>>>if (inList == 'NO'):
...     print ('Is not in list ')
... else:
...     print ('Is in list')
Is not in list
```

Here, we have set a flag 'inlist' initialized as 'NO' that we check after the loop is executed to know if the item is in a list or not. This structure of code is what the break and the else statement are designed for.

By implementing these two statements, the above code is optimized. First, the loop is stopped once the item is found in the list by inserting the break statement. Second, the else code will be displayed if the loop is run over all items and not found the item. In addition, we have fewer intermediate variables to handle. The optimized code with break and else statement is as follows:

```
>>> A = [20, 200, 2, 90]
>>> i = 0
>>> while (i < len (A)):
...        if (A [i] == 0): break
...        i = i+1
... else:
...        print ('Is not in the list')
Is not in the list
```

In the same manner, the for loop uses the else and break statements to exit the for loop when a condition is satisfied.

The complex form of the for loop is as follows:

```
for < i > in < data object >:
    block of code
    if < condition 1 or test 1 >:
        block of code 2
        break
    if < condition 2 or test 2 >:
        block of code 2
        continue
else:
    block of code 3
```

Like the while loop, when test 1 is evaluated to true, the for loop is exited and the else block is not run. When test 2 is evaluated to true, every statement that appears after is ignored and the loop goes to the header (i.e. evaluate the next item). Now that you understand the sophisticated format of the for loop, let's see some examples in an interactive session.

The following example is similar to the last example of the while loop. We search for an item in a list. This example illustrates also how to use nested loops.

We use the break and else statement to exit and return if the item is on the list.

```
>>> A = [20, 40, 90, 50, 60]
>>> B = [9, 90, 'no', 90, 20, 100]
>>>for j in B:
...     for i in A:
...         if j == i:
...             print ('Element', j, 'is in list')
...             break
...     else:
...         print ('Element', j, 'is not in list')
Element 20 is in list Element
    100 is not in list Element
    90 is in list Element
    100 is not in list Element
    100 is not in list
```

In this example, the first loop goes through the first list 'B's that stores the items being searched for and the second loop goes through the list that is being searched. Both loops are running together. When an item is found in list 'A', the second loop is exited. The else here is assigned to the second loop to return that the item is not the list.

The code presented here is just to present an illustration of using a break and else. This code can be optimized by using the 'in' operator that looks for any match in a sequence. The optimized code is as follows:

```
>>> A = [20, 40, 90, 50, 60]
>>> B = [9, 90, 'no', 90, 20, 100]
>>> for j in B:
...     if j in A:
...         print ('Element', j, 'is in list')
...     else:
...         print ('Element', j, 'is not in list')
Element 9 is not in list
Element 90 is in list
Element no is not in list
Element 90 is in list
Element 20 is in list
Element 100 is not in list
```

This code only works for the lists defined here. It would be helpful to be able to run the same code on other lists, too. This is when the function comes very handy. We will cover this topic in the next chapter. The loops we have covered in this section will also be used in chapter 8 of this book that covers files.

Indeed, loops are very handy to repeat the same task as long as it is necessary. Files come in the form of several lines that contains several characters. They are the typical use of the for loops. In chapter 8, we will cover how to use loops to read and write files.

Python Exceptions

Python exceptions are events that can have an impact or change the control flow of a script. Exceptions in Python are raised on errors. They can be raised and intercepted by the script. In Python, exceptions are handled using three statements that we will cover in this section.

The first statement try has two variations which are ' try/ finally ' and ' try/ except'. The first variation, 'try/ except', catches the exceptions and recovers from it by Python or by the user. The second variation, ' try/finally ', performs a clean-up whether the exception is raised or not. The second statement is ' raise ' and it triggers an exception in the code manually. The third statement is ' assert'. This statement raises an exception conditionally in the script. Now you must be wondering why to use exceptions in a script.

Exceptions are very handy in large programs to keep track if the code is running as expected. In other words, exceptions allow jumping pieces of code when something goes wrong.

Depending on what is expected from the program, when an exception is raised, the code might execute some tasks to recover from the exception that was raised or exit the code completely. In Python, exceptions are used for a wide range of purposes. Exceptions can be used to handle errors. Python is able to automatically trigger errors when it is running. These errors can be caught and assigned a code/task as a response or can be ignored. If the error is being ignored, Python would use the default handling of the error. The program will stop running and an error message will be displayed. Otherwise, if you develop a try statement as a response when the error is being raised, Python would ignore the default handling and would jump to your coded try statement. Hence, your script will continue running after the try.

Exceptions can also be used as a notification for events. In this context, exceptions are used as a validation condition signal without handling and coding flags that are processed in the program. For example, a routine that searches for a particular element might trigger an exception when failed instead of returning a Boolean or integer, as a result, to be tested after. Exceptions can serve to handle a special case.

A special case is a condition that can occur rarely. Instead of convoluting the code to take action, an exception can be inserted to take action when unusual cases occur. Exceptions can be used to stop actions. As mentioned before, the ' try/finally ' statement guarantees that code final closing tasks are executed whether an exception is raised or not during run time. Finally, the exceptions can be used as flow control similar to a ' goto ' statement available in other programming languages. Now that you got the general idea behind exceptions, let's try some examples in the interactive session.

Try/except statement

The syntax for this exception statement is in the following form:

```
try:
 statement or task to run
except < name >:
 statement
```

In order to illustrate the ' try/except ' statement, let's consider a function that we will run as a task in the try block. We define a function that takes as input two arguments where the first is a list and the second is an index. This function returns the element of the index passed as a second argument. Don't worry about functions at this step. We will cover them in more detail in the next chapter.

```
>>>def fct (myList, ind):
...     return (myList[ind])
```

Now, if we try to call this function with the list and the index defined below, we get something like:

```
>>> myList = [20, 40, 50, 70]
>>> ind = 3
>>> A = fct (myList, ind)
>>> print (' element is: ', A)
element is: 70
```

Now, if we try to pass an index equal to superior to 3, Python will throw an error as follows:

```
>>> ind = 8
>>> A = fct (myList, ind)
Traceback (most recent call last):
File "<stdin>", line 1, in <module>
File "<stdin>", line 2, in fct
IndexError: list index out of range
```

Python detects automatically that the index passed is out of the range of the list indices. Then, it raises an error handled by the default IndexError exception which prints a message error along with the number of the lines where the error occurred.

Here we are working in an interactive session, so the lines are not meaningful. If real applications where the program is not run in the interactive session, the program will be stopped from execution by the default top handler. Python throws this error because it is not being raised by the defined function. You can also try to catch the exception when running the function and not trigger the default Python hander using the ' try/except ' statement. The code will be, in this case, to run the function as follows:

```
>>> try:
...     fct (myList, 9)
... except IndexError:
...     print (' This is an exception')
...
This is an exception
>>>
```

In this case, Python ignores the default handler and jumps to the defined handler. The try has stopped the function from running. Then Python displays >>> in the prompt which means it is ready to run statement.

In more complex programs and real applications, to recover and catch from the exceptions, you can use the try statement. Then, we would define something like:

```
>>> def catcher():
...     try:
...             fct (myList, 9)
...     except IndexError:
...             print (' This is an exceptions')
... print (' Will continue running')
...
>>> catcher()
This is an exception
Will continue running
>>>
```

Now, the exception is being raised by try, and the program continued running after the exception by printing the message ' Will continue running'. The program resumes normally and runs the following statements.

Try /finally statement

In this sub-section, we illustrate how the ' try/finally ' works. The ' try/finally ' syntax is similar to the ' try/exception ' syntax and is in the form presented below:

```
try:
    statement or task to run
finally:
    statement or task to run
```

This exception statement runs the code assigned to finally, whether try raised an exception or not.

```
>>> Mylist = [20, 300, 900, 90]
>>> ind = 2
>>> try:
...      fct (Mylist, ind)
... finally:
...      print (' This is the finally block')
...
900
This is the finally block
```

Here the finally block is launched with the try block that runs normally without any exception being raised and the script continued running after the try block. This code is similar to displaying the message in the finally block after running the function. So, the code is similar to the following statements:

```
>>> ind = 2
>>> myList = [20, 300, 900, 90]
>>> fct(myList, ind)
900
>>> print ('This is the finally block')
This is the finally block
```

However, in a real application where the code is run outside of the interactive session if the function triggers an exception every code statement after it is not executed. So, we might try a code that resumes after the try statement if something went wrong. For example,

```
>>> def after():
...     try:
...         fct (myList, 9)
...     finally:
...         print ('This is the finally block')
...     print ('This the block after try and finally')
...
>>> after()
This is the finally block
Traceback (most recent call last):
  File "<stdin>", line 1, in <module>
  File "<stdin>", line 3, in after
  File "<stdin>", line 2, in fct
IndexError: list index out of range
```

Now, you can notice the code did not display the message 'This the block after try and finally'. The reason is that the control flow does not continue when an exception is triggered in the try/finally statement. Python executes the code assigned to finally. Then it propagates the error raised in the try section through the code to the default handler in this case. If the function call is changed for a case where it does not raise an error, the code after the try/finally would run. The code below shows an example:

```
>>> def after():
...     try:
...         fct(myList,0)
...     finally:
...         print ('This the finally block')
...     print ('This the block after try and finally')
...
>>> after()
This the finally block
This the block after try and finally
```

Chapter 5: Functions in Python

This chapter of the book covers functions that are a piece of code that can be executed repeatedly with different variables to generate a different outcome. We have been already using this notion in the previous chapters whether it is using Python's built-in function like print() to display a message in standard output of Python or the function that we defined in the section illustrating exceptions. This chapter makes the emphasis on how to develop functions that compute and return values and how to code a script to be reused easily.

Function Utilities in Programming

Functions are a fundamental concept in any programming language. They are also known as procedures or routines in other programming languages. Functions are very handy when you need to run the same code with different variable values.

For instance, you want to compute the factorial of different numbers. Instead of coding the same code for each number, you would define a function that takes as input the number of interests, computes its factorial, and returns the result. This way you just have to call the same function for each number inside a loop for instance.

In this context, functions serve for two main purposes. The first is to make the code reusable. They provide a way to package your code such that it is used more than once or in multiple places in the same or different program. So far, illustrations and code examples presented in this book are run immediately in the interactive session. With functions, the code can be wrapped and generalized to be used several times after. The second purpose of functions is to decompose a program into several pieces where each piece is assigned a role. This is very useful when coding a large program or a framework that replicates the functioning of a complex system. Functions allow us to break down the system into pieces where each piece is coded by a function. Each function would serve to perform a task in a large system.

This way of coding makes it easy to implement complex systems than just implementing a whole system in one chunk of code. You can think of functions as a procedure that allows replicating how to do something. Coding functions does not imply different syntax. In the following sections, we will cover the keywords and the basics to develop functions with Python.

Function Concept, Declaration and Calling in Python

We have been using and calling functions that are built-in Python in the earlier chapters of this book. For example, to compute the length of an object, we call the function len. In this section, we are going to learn how to define new functions. Every new function you define in Python works exactly the same as the built-in functions of Python. Functions are called through statements or expressions and can take input arguments and return a result. Developing new functions requires using additional statements that were presented in table 5 shown in Chapter 4.

In Python, functions act differently compared to complied programming languages (e.g. C or C++).

'def ', a new statement, defines the Python functions. This is also an executable code. When you develop a new function, it is not recognized by the Python until it hits a 'def ' statement and runs through it. Sometimes, the 'def ' statement is inserted in if test or a loop or maybe inside other 'def ' statement. In a real application, the 'def ' statements are defined within modules. When the module is imported in the Python environment workspace, the functions are generated automatically. We will cover modules in more detail in the next chapter. The 'def ' statement makes a new object (i.e. a function) and assigns a name to it. A function object is created and given a name every time a 'def ' statement is found by Python. This name is the reference of the function which can be saved in a list or given another name. Functions can send back an object result after they are called. When Python goes through a statement that calls a function, it runs through the function code until it finishes. Then it resumes to the following statements.

If a function returns a value, it communicates it back to the control flow as a return statement. This result is then the outcome of calling this function. Functions can take optionally input arguments that passed as a reference.

Unlike other programming languages such as C or C++, references (i.e. variables) are shared across the function and Python called. This means that a variable that is modified within a function is also modified automatically within the entire code. In other words, if you define a variable name outside a function. Then, later in the code, you call a function that shares the same variable name (i.e. reference) that changes its values. When the function is finished running and the control is given back to the controller, the variable has the same value that was assigned inside the function and not the value that was assigned before the function call. As we have mentioned in Chapter 2, variables that are assigned inside a function are, by default, local variables. They are defined only inside the function. Once the function finishes running, these variables don't exist anymore.

Like any other object data, the function does not need any declaration of any kind prior to use. Inputs arguments, as well as output arguments, can be of any type of data object. Hence, the functions can be called with different data types.

To create a new function, we use the 'def ' statement with the following syntax:

>   def < function name> (argument 1, ..., argument n):
>   statements or tasks to perform

Like any compound statement in Python, indentation is very imported. All statements that constitute the function body should be intended unless it is one single statement that can appear after the header (i.e. after the colon). The function body is executed every time the function is called. After 'def ' is the name of the function which attributed to reference to the function object, followed by the arguments.

The name of arguments is attributed to the data object that is passed to the function when called.

If no argument is to be passed to the function, then the syntax is as follows:

> def < function name> ():
> > statements or tasks to perform

Usually, a function returns an output argument or statement. In this case, the syntax of the function includes a return statement as follow:

> def < function name> (argument 1, ..., argument n):
> > statements or tasks to perform
> > return < output value>

In Python, the 'def ' can appear anywhere in the code, even inside other statement. For example, we can define a function according to a test like follows:

> If < condition >:
> > def my_function():
> > > statement 1
>
> else:
> > def my_function(argument):
> > > statement 2

In the syntax example given above, the function my_function is defined with or without input argument depending on whether the condition is satisfied or not. The 'def ' statement works as any Python assignment statement and the function is not defined until the code goes through the 'def ' statement. The function name can also be changed anytime by assigning it to another name. For instance, we can do:

    Name2= my_function

To call a function we just type in the name of the function with arguments if it takes any.

    function_name (argument 1, argument 2, ..., argument 3)
Or   function_name ()

In the following sections of this chapter, we are going to present explicitly how functions use arguments and return values with some examples.

Function Expressions, Arguments, and Returned outputs

As we have seen in the previous section, arguments of a function, also called parameters, are passed between parenthesis. When the function is called, Python uses these arguments to reference the date object passed as input. There is no requirement to declare the type of the data object that the function is expecting as input. Usually, functions are defined within modules and run outside of the interactive session. For the sake of simplicity and the fact we are using simple basic examples, the interactive prompt would be sufficient to run the examples of this book.

The following code is an example of a function that takes as an argument a number, computes and displays a factorial of a number.

```
>>> def Xfactorial (X):
...     P = 1
...     for i in range (1, X + 1):
...         P *= i
...     print ('Factorial of ', X, 'is:', P)
```

Now, to call this function, we simply type the name of the function with the number for which we want to compute the factorial. For example:

```
>>> Xfactorial (3)
Factorial of 3 is: 6
```

If we want to save the output of this function in a later use in the code, we use the return statement when defining the function as follows:

```
>>> def Xfactorial (X):
...     P = 1
...     for i in range (1, X + 1):
...         P *= i
...     return P
```

Then when calling the function, we assign the function to a variable as follows:

```
>>> A = Xfactorial (3)
>>> print ('Factorial 3 is:', A)
Factorial 3 is: 6
```

Now, let's consider a simple function that returns the value of X times Y with X and Y two input arguments.

>>> def Prod (A, B):
...   return A * B

Now, let's call this function with input arguments of different types.

>>> A = Prod (2, 3)
>>> print ('This is an example of calling the Prod function with two integers:', A)
This is an example of calling the Prod function with two integers: 6
>>> A = Prod (1.5, 3)
>>> print ('This is an example of calling the Prod function with a float and integer:', A)
This is an example of calling the Prod function with a float and integer: 4.5
>>> A = Prod ('name', 3)
>>> print ('This is an example of calling the Prod function with a string and integer\n:', A)
This is an example of calling the Prod function with a string and integer: namenamename
>>> A = Prod ('name', 'name')
Traceback (most recent call last):
 File "<stdin>", line 1, in <module>
 File "<stdin>", line 2, in Prod
TypeError: can't multiply sequence by non-int of type 'str'

In the examples above, we called the function and passed two integers, a float and integer, and a string and an integer. In the first case, it returned an integer. In the second, it returned a float, and in the third, it returned a string. In the final example, we passed two strings input arguments and Python raised an error because multiplication between strings does not exit. Overall, there is no declaration or restriction on the data type that can be passed to a function as long as the operations in the function body are defined.

Overall, Python functions allow defining code scripts that are reusable as many times as it is needed. There are no restrictions on the data object type passed as arguments. The code becomes general and used in any context as long as the operations inside the function are defined. Moreover, you can define your own operations inside these functions or include exception statements that can handle issues in this case. By coding a script within a function, it makes it easy to make a modification if needed and to be made in one single place. You can also insert a function code within a module file.

This way, the function can be imported by importing the module and used within any program or shared with other programs for wide broad use. In fact, this is exactly how packages are developed and used in Python. In the next chapter, we are going to cover this specific topic on how to develop modules with Python.

Chapter 6: Modules in Python

Modules, also known as packages, are a set of names. This is usually a library of functions and/or object classes that are made available to be used within different programs. We used the notion of modules earlier in this chapter to use some function from the math library. In this chapter, we are going to cover in-depth on how to develop and define modules. In order to use modules in a Python program, the following statements are used: import, from, reload. The first one imports the whole module. The second allows import only a specific name or element from the module. The third one, reload, allows reloading a code of a module while Python is running and without stopping in it. Before digging into their definition and development, let's start first by the utility of modules or packages within Python.

Modules Concept and Utility Within Python

Modules are a very simple way to make a system component organized. Basically, modules allow reusing the same code over and over. So far, we were working in a Python interactive session. Every code we have written and tested is lost once we exit the interactive session. Modules are saved in files that make them persistent, reusable, and sharable. You can consider modules as a set of files where you can define functions, names, data objects, attributes, and so on. Modules are a tool to group several components of a system in a single place. In Python programming, modules are among the highest-level unit. They point to the name of packages and tools. In addition, they allow the sharing of the implemented data. You only need one copy of the module to be able to use across a large program. If an object is to be used in different functions and programs, coding it as a module allows share it with other programmers.

To have a sense of the architecture of Python coding, we go through some general structure explanation.

We have been using so far in this book very simple code examples that do not really have high-level structure. In large applications, a program is a set of several Python files. By Python files, we mean files that contain Python code and have a .py extension. There is one main high-level program and the other files are the modules. The high-level file consists of the main code that dictates the control flow and executes the application. Module files define the tools that are needed to process elements and components of the main program and maybe elsewhere. The main program makes use of the tools that are specified in the modules.

In their turn, modules make use of tools that are specified in other modules. When you import a module in Python, you have access to every tool that is declared or defined in that specific module. Attributes are the variables or the functions associated with the tools within a module. Hence, when a module is imported, we have access to the attributes of the tools as well to process them. For instance, let's consider we have two Python files named file1.py and file2.py where the file1.py is the main program and file2.py is the module. In the file2.py, we have a code that defines the following function that we have used in the previous chapter:

>   def Xfactorial (X):
>   P = 1
>   for i in range (1, X + 1):
>   P *= i
>   return P

In order to use this function in the main program, we should define code statements in the file1.py as follows:

>   Import file2
>   A = file2.Xfactorial (3)

The first line imports the module file2.py. This statement means to load the file file2.py. This gives access to the file1.py to all tools and functions defined in file2.py by the name file2. The function Xfactorial is called by the second line. The module file2.py is where this function is defined using the attributes' syntax.

The line file2.Xfactorial() means fetch any name value of Xfactorial and lies within the code body of file2. In this example, it is a function that is callable. So, we have provided an input argument and assigned the output result to the variable A. If we add a third statement to print the variable A and run the file file1.py, it would display 6 which is the factorial of 3. Along Python, you will see the attribute syntax as object.attribute. This basically allows calling the attributes that might be a function or data object that provides properties of the object.

Note that some modules that you might import when programming with Python are available in Python itself. As we have mentioned at the beginning of this book, Python comes with a standard large library that has built-in modules. These modules support all common tasks that might be needed in programming from operating system interfaces to graphical user interface. They are not part of the language. However, they can be imported and comes with a software installation package.

You can check the complete list of available modules in a manual that comes with the installation or goes to the official Python website: www.Python.org. This manual is kept updated every time a new version of Python is released.

How to Import a Module

We have talked about importing a module without really explaining what happens behind in Python. Imports are a very fundamental concept in Python programming structure. In this section, we are going to cover in-depth how really Python imports modules within a program. In fact, Python follows three steps to import a file or a module within the work environment of a program. The first step consists of finding the file that contains the module. The second step consists of compiling the module to a byte-code if required. Finally, the third step runs the code within the module file in order to build the objects that are defined. These three steps are run only when the module is imported for the first time during the execution of a program. This module and all its objects are loaded in the memory. When the module is imported further in the program, it skips all three steps and just fetch the objects defined by the module and are saved in memory.

At the very first step of importing a module, Python has to find the module file location.

Note that, so far in the examples we presented, we used import without providing the complete path of the module or extension .py. We just used import math, or import file2.py (an example of the previous section). Python import statement omits the extension and the path. We just simply import a module by its name. The reason for this is that Python has a module that looks for paths called 'search path module'. This module is used specifically to find the path of module files that are imported by the import statements.

In some cases, you might need to configure the path search of modules in order to be able to use new modules that are not part of the standard library. You need to customize it in order to include these new modules. The search path is simply the concatenation of the home directory, directories of PYTHONPATH, directories of the standard library, and optionally if the content of files with extension .pth when they exist. The home directory is set automatically by the system to a directory of Python executable when launched from the interactive session, or it can be modified to the working directory where your program is saved.

This directory is the first to be searched when import a module is run without a path. Hence, if your home directory points to a directory that includes your program along with the modules, importing these modules does not require any path specification.

The directory of the standard library is also searched automatically. This directory contains all default libraries that come with Python. The directories of PYTHONPATH can be set in order to point toward the directory of new modules that are developed. In fact, PTYHONPATH is an environment variable that contains a list of directories that contains Python files. When PTYHONPATH is set, all these paths are included in the Python environment and the search path directory would search these directories too when importing modules. Python also allows defining a file with .pth extension that contains directories, one in each line. This file serves the same as PTYHONPATH when included appropriately in a directory. You can check the directories' paths included when you run Python using sys.path. You simply print sys.path to get the list of the directories that Python will be searching for.

Remember, when importing a module, we just use the name of the module without its extension. When Python is searching for a module in its environment paths, it selects the first name that matches the module name regardless of the extension. Because Python allows using packages that are coded in other languages, it does not simply select a module with .py extension but a file name or even a zip file name that matches the module name being imported. Therefore, you should name your modules distinctly and configure the search path in a manner that makes it obvious to choose a module.

When Python finds the source code of the module file with a name that corresponds to the name in the import statement, it will compile it into byte code in case it is required. This step is skipped if Python finds an already byte code file with no source code. If the source code has been modified, another byte code file is automatically regenerated by Python while the program runs in other further executions. Byte code files have typically .pyc extension.

When Python is searching and finds the module file name, it will load the byte code file that corresponds to the latest version of the source code with .py extension. If the source code is newer than the byte code file, it will generate a new one by compiling the source code file. Note that only imported files have corresponding files with .pyc extension. These files, the byte code files, are stored on your machine to make the imports faster in future use.

The third step of the import statement is running the module's byte code. Each statement and each assignment in the file are executed. This allows generating any function, data objects, and so on defined in the module. The functions and all attributes are accessed within the program via importers. During this step, you will see print statements if they exist. The 'def ' statement will create a function object to be used in the main program.

To summarize the import statement, involve searching for the file, compiling it, and running the byte code file. All other imports statement uses the module stored in memory and ignore all the three steps.

When first imported, Python will look in the search path module to select the module. Hence, it is important to configure correctly the path environment variable to point to the directory that contains new defined modules. Now that you have the big picture and the concept of modules, let's explore how we can define and develop new modules.

How to write and use a module in Python?

Modules in Python can be created very easily and do not require any specific syntax. Modules are simply files with a .py extension that contains Python code. You can use a text editor like Notepad++ to develop and write modules then save them in files with the .py extension. Then, you just import these files like we have seen in the previous section to make use of the contained code.

When you create a module, all the data object including functions that are defined becomes the module attributes. These attributes are accessed and used via the attribute syntax like follows: module.attribute. For instance, if we define a module named ' MyModule.py ' that has the following function:

```
def Myfct (A):
    print (' A by 2 is: ', A * 2)
    return A * 2
```

The function ' Myfct ' becomes the attribute of the module ' MyModule.py '. Basically, you can call a module any Python code that you develop and save in a file with a .py extension if you are importing them in later use. Module names are referenced variables. Hence, when naming a module, you should follow the same rules as for variable naming. You might be able to name your module anything you want. But if the rules are not respected, Python throws an error. For instance, if you name your module $2P.py, you will not be able to import it and Python would trigger a syntax error. Directory names that contain the module and Python packages should follow the same rules. In addition, their names cannot contain any space. In the rest of this section, we are going to provide some code examples of defining and using modules.

There are two statements that can be employed to make use of a module. The first one is the import statement we have covered in the previous section. Let's consider again the previous example to illustrate a module 'MyModule.py' that contains ' Myfct' function:

```
def Myfct(A):
    print (A, 'by 2 is: ', A * 2)
```

Now, to use this module, we import it using the following statements:

>>> import MyModule
>>> MyModule.Myfct(2)
2 by 2 is: 4

Now, the MyModule name is being used by Python to load the file and as a variable in the program. The module name should be used to access all its attributes. Another way to import and use a module attribute is by using the 'from import' statement. This statement works in the same manner as the import statement we have been using. Instead of using the module name to fetch for its attributes, we can access the attributes by their names directly. For example:

>>> from MyModule import Myfct
>>> Myfct (2)
2 by 2 is: 4

Basically, this statement makes a copy of the function name without using the module name. There is another form of 'from import' statement that uses an *. This statement allows copying all names that are assigned to objects in the module. For example:

>>> from MyModule import *
>>> Myfct (2)
2 by 2 is: 4

Because modules names become variables (i.e. references to objects), Python supports importing a module with an alias. Then we can access its attributes using the alias instead of its name. For instance, we can attribute an alias to our module like follows:

>>> import Mymodule as md
>>> md.Myfct(2)
2 by 2 is: 4

Data objects other than functions are accessed the same way with attribute syntax. For instance, we can define and initialize data objects in modules than used them later in the program. Let's consider the following code to create a module named ExModule.py.

    A = 9
    Name = 'John'

In this example, we initialize both variables A and Name. Now, after importing the module, we can get both variables as follows:

```
>>> import ExModule
>>> print ('A is: ', ExModule.A)
A is: 9
>>> print ('Name is: ', Exmodule.Name)
Name is: John
```

Or we can assign the attributes to other variables. For instance:

```
>>> import ExModule
>>> B = ExModule.A
>>> print ('B is: ', B)
B is: 9
```

If we use the 'from import' statement to import the attributes, the names of the attributes become variables in the script. For example:

```
>>> from Exmodule import A, Name
>>> print ('A is: ', A, 'and Name is: ', Name)
A is 9 and Name is John
```

Note that from the import statement supports importing multiple attributes in one single line. Python allows changing objects that are sharable.

For instance, let's consider the following code to define the module named ExModul1.py:

```
A = 9
MyList = [ 90, 40, 80]
```

Now, let's import this module and try to change the values of the attributes to see how Python behaves.

```
>>> from ExModule1 import A, MyList
>>> A = 20
>>> myList [ 0] = 100
```

Now, let's re-import the module and print those two attributes and see what changes Python has made.

```
>>> import ExModule1
>>> print (' A is: ', ExModule1.A)
A is: 9
>>> print ('My list is: ', ExModule.myList)
My list is: [100, 40, 80]
```

You can notice that Python has changed the value of the first element of the list but did not change the value of the variable 'A' to the value we assigned before. The reason is that when a mutable object like lists is changed locally, the changes apply also in the module from which they were imported. Reassigning a fetched variable name does not reassign the reference in the module from which it was imported. In fact, there is no link between the reference variable name copied and the file it was copied from. In order to make a valid modification in the script and the module it is imported from, we should use the import statement like follows:

>>> import ExModule1
>>> ExModule1.A = 200

The difference between changing the attributes 'A' and 'myList' is the fact that 'A' is a variable name and 'myList' is an object data. That is why modification to the variable 'A' should use import to be applied in the module file, too.

We have mentioned that importing a module for the first time in a script implies going through three steps that are searching for the module, compiling the module, and running the module. All other imports of the module later in the script skip all these three steps and access to module loaded in the memory. Now, let's try an example to see how this really works. Consider we have a module with the following code and named ExModule2.py:

```
print (' Hello World\n')
print (' This is my first module in Python')
A = 9
```

Now, let's import this module and see how Python behaves when importing this module:

```
>>> import ExModule2
Hello World
This is my first module in Python
>>>
```

You can notice that when importing this module, it displays both messages. Now, let's try to reassign a value to the attribute ' A', then re-import the module with the import statement.

```
>>> ExModule.A = 100
>>> import Exmodule2
>>>
```

As you can note from the example, Python did not display the messages, ' Hello World' and ' This is my first module in Python' because it did not re-run the module. It just used the module that is already loaded in the memory.

In order to make Python really goes through all steps of importing a module for the second time in a script, we should use the reload statement. When using this statement, we force Python to import the module as it would for the first time. In addition, it helps make modifications in the program while it is running without interrupting it. It also helps see instantly the modifications that are made.

The reload is actually a function and not a statement in Python that takes as argument a module that is already loaded in memory.

Because reload is a function and expects an argument, this argument should be already assigned an object which is a module object. If for some reason the import statement failed to import a module, you will not be able to reload it. You have to repeat the import statement until it imports the module successfully. Like any other function, the reload takes the module name reference between parenthesis. The general form of using reload with import is as follows:

```
import module_name
list of statements that use module attributes
reload(module_name)
list of statements that use module attributes
```

The module object is changed by the reload function. Hence, any reference to that module in your scripts is impacted by the reload function. Those statements that use the module attributes will be using the values of the new attributes if they are modified.

The reload function overwrites the module source code and re-runs it instead of deleting the file and creating a new one. In the following code example, we will see a concrete illustration of the reload functioning. We consider the following code to create a module named ExModule3.py:

```
my_message = ' This is my module first version'
def display ():
    print (my_message)
```

This module simply assigns a string to the variable 'my_message' and print it. Now, let's import this module in Python and call the attribute function:

```
>>> import ExModule3
>>> Exmodule3.display()
This is my module first version
>>>
```

Now, go to your text editor and edit the module source code without stopping the Python prompt shell. You can make a change as follows:

> my_message = ' This is my module second version edited in the text editor'
> def display ():
>   print (my_message)

Now, back to the interactive session of Python in the prompt shell, you can try to import the module and call the function:

> \>>> import ExModule3
> \>>> Exmodule3.display()
> This is my module first version
> \>>>

As you can notice that the message did not change although the source code file was modified. As said before, all imports after the first import use the already loaded module in memory.

To get the new message and access the modification made in the module, we use the reload function:

>>> reload (ExModule3)
<module 'ExModule3)>
>>> Exmodule3.display()
This is my module second version edited in the text editor

Note that the reload function re-runs module and returns the module object. Because it was executed in the interactive session, it displays < module name> by default.

Chapter 7: Python Debugging

In some cases, a program is developed, but when running, it does not provide the desired outcome or it gets stuck somewhere in the workflow. This implies that the program should be scrutinized while it is running on a test in order to get a sense of where the program should be corrected or where things go wrong. This action is what is named by programmers debugging. This task is actively used in order to make sure that a program is running as it is supposed to be. In this chapter, we will cover this topic and present the commands that are available to debug Python programs. First, let's talk in-depth about what is debugging.

What is debugging?

Debugging is simply the process of finding and fixing errors in a program. Debugging verifies the functioning of a program to fix statements of operations that make the program stack and not running appropriately.

The simplest and most obvious way to debug a program is using the print function in order to spot the output of functions or variables. In general, the print allows getting information to have a look inside of the functioning of the program. However, this method has several drawbacks. The major is that you need to add changes to the code several times in order to add the print in places where you need to extract information. These places are commonly known as breakpoints. Then you have to run the program every time. There are some advanced debugger tools that can be used. These tools mostly are very efficient and allow saving a great amount of time when used compared to debugging with print.

Python has a debugger that comes by default with the software when installed. This debugger is simply a tool that gives ways to get a look at the code while it is running. When using this tool, you can make changes instantly in the code and alter the values of the variables all while you run the code in chunks. The debugger that comes with Python is named pdb. This tool is in the form of a command-line interface.

This debugger, as any package, is imported with the import statement in order to be able to use it.

> import pdb, pdb.set_trace.

In order to be used, the debugger should be imported into the program you wish to debug. When Python interpreter runs this line, you will be redirected to a prompt command on your terminal in which the program is launched. Typically, this is the prompt of Python with commands that allows you to evaluate your code. We cover the list of these commands in the following section.

Python Debugger Commands

Python default debugger has several debugging commands which are presented in the table below. Here we cover the most basic one. The first command, list, allows you to list the line where the control workflow is on. You can check specific parts of your code by passing their first and last lines as arguments to the list command. You can also check the code around a specific line bypassing only the number of this line to the list command. The up and down commands allow navigating around the code of your program. By using these commands, you are able to know which statement is calling the function that is currently running or understand reasons why the interpreter is behaving or running certain code parts. The next and step are commands that allow resuming execution of the code line by line. The next command will jump to the following line of the function that is currently running even if it calls another function. On the contrary, the step function allows you to go deeper in the code chain rather than just executing the following line.

Finally, the break is a command that enables adding new breakpoints with no requirements to make any modifications in the source code.

Table 9: List Python debugger commands

Debug command	Explanation
Alias or a	allows creating an alias to the command
args or rgs	allows showing the list of arguments
break or b	allows setting breakpoints.
disable	allows disabling breakpoints supplied as a list separated by a space
ignore	allows setting a count for a number of breakpoints
commands	allows specifying a command list for a number of breakpoints
continue or c or cont	continue running the code until it reaches a breakpoint
exit	quit the debugger
interact	launch an interpreter that is interactive
list or l	allows showing the code for specific lines
next or n	resumes execution until the following line of the function currently running

restart	allows restarting the program
step or s	run expression in the current line
unalias	removes alias
where or w	displays a trace of the recent last frame
down or d	goes to the next line down
up or u	goes to the above line
clear or cl	allows clearing all breakpoints
enable	allows enabling breakpoints
condition	allows setting conditions for breakpoints as a test that should be evaluated to true in order to set the breakpoint
p	allows evaluating the expression in the current line
help or h	If no argument is supplied, displays list of commands, otherwise, displays information about the command passed as an argument
jump or j	allows setting the number of the line to run next; it allows jumping code parts or running the code from the start
longlist or ll	allows showing the whole code for the function currently running
quit or q	exit the debugger and abort the program

return or r	continue running the code until hits a function return
tbreak	allows making a temporary breakpoint
until or ill	if no argument is passed, it continues running the code until a line which has a number superior to the current is reached
whatis	displays the expression type

Now that you know the concept behind debugging and its basic commands, let's see a real example. We consider the following code saved in a file named test.py.

```
def Myfct1 (A):
    print ('A by 2 is:', A * 2)
return A * 2

def Myfct2 (B, A):
    C = B * A
A = 4
B = 'name'
Myfct2 (B, A)
```

You can notice that this code does not import Python debugger, the pdb module.

Instead, we are going to launch the function in the prompt with Python in a debugger mode with the following command:

>   C:\Users***\Desktop>Python -m pdb test.py
>   > c:\users***\desktop\test.py(1)<module>()
>   -> def Myfct (A):
>   (Pdb)

As you can see, Python did not return the usual >>> in the prompt but it returned instead (Pdb). This means that the debugger is waiting for debugger commands. Now, let's test some of the commands listed in Table 9 above to get a sense of how the debugger works.

We start by the list command.

```
(Pdb) list
1 -> def Myfct1(A):
2  print ('A by 2 is:', A * 2)
3  return A * 2
4
5 def Myfct2(B, A):
6  C = B * A
7
8 A = 4
9 B = 'name'
10 Myfct2(B, A)
[EOF]
```

In this example, we applied the list command with no argument. It returned the content of the file with line numbers. If we pass arguments (i.e. line numbers) to the list command, it will return only the code that shows between these lines. For instance:

```
(Pdb) list 2, 3
2  print ('A by 2 is:', A * 2)
3  return A * 2
(Pdb)
```

If we use now the next command it will return, the next line after where the current curser is:

> (Pdb) next
> > c:\users***\desktop\test.py(5)<module>()
> -> def Myfct2(B, A):
> (Pdb)

We skip lines in the debugger using the jump command as follows:

> (Pdb) jump 8
> > c:\users*****\desktop\test.py(8)<module>()
> -> A = 4
> (Pdb)

If we try to print the variable 'A', Python will display a name error because this statement is not yet executed.

The curser is just pointing to this line:

> (Pdb) A
> *** NameError: name 'A' is not defined
> (Pdb)

Now, in order to print variable names, we should actually run the program with commands that actually run the program not just show its content. Among these commands is the continue command.

So, let's run now the continue command:

> (Pdb) continue
> Traceback (most recent call last):
>   File "C:\Users****\Anaconda3\lib\pdb.py", line 1697, in main
>   pdb._runscript(mainpyfile)
>   File "C:\Users****\Anaconda3\lib\pdb.py", line 1566, in _runscript
>   self.run(statement)
>   File "C:\Users****\Anaconda3\lib\bdb.py", line 585, in run
>   exec (cmd, globals, locals)
>   File "<string>", line 1, in <module>
>   File "c:\users****\desktop\test.py", line 8, in <module>
>   A = 4
> NameError: name 'Myfct2' is not defined
> Uncaught exception. Entering post mortem debugging
> Running 'cont' or 'step' will restart the program
> > c:\users*****\desktop\test.py(8)<module>()
> -> A = 4

Now, here that the continue launched different built-in functions of the debugger. It finally displayed an Error name for the 'Myfct2' because the 'def' statement of this function was not executed.

Now, if we try to print the value of the variable ' A ', we get:

```
(Pdb) A
4
(Pdb)
```

If we reach the bottom of the file and run, for instance, the next command, Python debugger returns:

```
(Pdb) next
Post mortem debugger finished. The test.py will be restarted
> c:\users\***\desktop\test.py(1)<module>()
-> def Myfct1(A):
```

The longlist command allows showing the entire code. For instance:

```
(Pdb) longlist
1 -> def Myfct1 (A):
2  print ('A by 2 is:', A*2)
3  return A * 2
4
5 def Myfct2 (B, A):
6  C = B * A
7
8 A = 4
9 B = 'name'
10 Myfct2(B, A)
(Pdb)
```

Now, to run a code, we use the command step. For instance, let's quit the debugger with the command q() and restarted it again to test the command step.

> (Pdb) q()
> C:\Users****\Desktop>Python -m pdb test.py
> > c:\users****\desktop\test.py(1)<module>()
> -> def Myfct1 (A):
> (Pdb) step
> > c:\users****\desktop\test.py(5)<module>()
> -> def Myfct2 (B, A):
> (Pdb)

As you can notice, when a step command is run, the current line is def Myfct2 (B, A). This means that it is executed the 'def' statement of the first function. We can test that by calling this function:

> (Pdb) Myfct1 (3)
> A by 2 is: 6
> 6
> (Pdb)

We can also pass an argument to step function to specify which line to run. For instance, we pass as argument Line 8. The debugger will run everything before line 8. As we can see from the example below, we can both print the variable A and call the function Myfct2 because these statements were both executed.

```
(Pdb) step 8
> c:\users\****\desktop\test.py(8)<module>()
-> B = 'name'
(Pdb) A
4
 (Pdb) Myfct2 (5, 3)
(Pdb)
```

Because we have reached the end of the file, let's use continue to go back to the beginning of the file and test other commands.

```
(Pdb) cont
The program finished and will be restarted
> c:\users\****\desktop\test.py(1)<module>()
-> def Myfct1 (A):
```

As you can see when running continue command at the end file, the debugger shows a message that lets you know that the program has finished and it is restarting. Now, we are going to test the whatis command:

> (Pdb) whatis 2
> <class 'int'>
> (Pdb)

This command returns the type of the data object of the expression that appears in the Line passed as an argument.

Now, let's set some breakpoints using the command break.

> (Pdb) break 3
> Breakpoint 1 at c:\users*****\desktop\test.py:3
> (Pdb)

This command displays a message regarding where the breakpoint was added along with the Python file. We can clear breakpoints with the clear command. After running this command, the debugger will display a message that asks whether you want to clear all breaks or not. Then it prints a message to confirm that the breakpoint was deleted along with the path of the Python file.

> (Pdb) clear
> Clear all breaks? Y
> Deleted breakpoint 1 at c:\users****\desktop\test.py:3
> (Pdb)

If you run a longlist after adding a breakpoint in your Python script, it will show you where the breakpoint was added. So, you don't have to go check in your Text Editor.

For instance, we add a break in line number 2:

```
(Pdb) break 2
Breakpoint 2 at c:\users\****\desktop\test.py:2
(Pdb) longlist
1 def Myfct1 (A):
2 B print ('A by 2 is:', A * 2)
3 return A * 2
4
5 def Myfct2 (B, A):
6 C = B * A
7 A = 4
8 B = 'name'
9 -> Myfct2 (B,A)
(Pdb)
```

To resume this chapter, using debugger tools are very efficient to get a look inside of the program while it is running. It let you know what's going on when the program is running without having to make any changes in its source code. In addition, you can see all the changes you make and breakpoints you add while you are debugging with the Python module pdb.

Moreover, this Python default debugger has numerous commands listed in Table 9 that allows an efficient scrutinization of your code.

Chapter 8: Files in Python

Files are a wide notion that is used to call any storage of your computer and handled by the operating system. Files are used to store data and information. When programming, you need tools that extract this information from the files or tools to save processed information in a file. In this chapter, we are going to cover how to handle files in Python.

Reading and writing files in Python

In Python, files are considered as a data object. In fact, Python has a built-in data object type assigned specifically for files. Unlike other data types we have seen in chapter 3, the file data object is associated only with common methods used to process files. The built-in method open is a function that allows creating a file data object to be processed. In short, this method links the file data object to the file stored in the hardware of your machine. Once you call open function, you have access to the file in order to read it or write it using the read and write attributes of the file data object.

Table 10 presented below lists all common methods used to process files. In order to read a file, the function open is called with file name along with the mode to process the file which is 'r' in this case. To write a file, the process mode is 'w'. This mode creates a new file. If a file exists with the same name used to open a file in a writing mode, it will be overwritten. In order to write or add content into the existing file, the file should be open with mode append (i.e. 'a'). The file name can include or not the file path of the directory that contains or will contain the file. If the path is not specified, then Python would assume that the file is in the working directory which is the directory where the current program is running.

Table 10: List methods to process files.

Method	Explanation
File2Read = open (file_path/file_name, 'r')	Defines a file data object to write
File2write = open (file_path/file_name, 'w')	Defines a file data object to read
content = File2read.read()	Reads the whole file and assign the content to a single string
content = File2read.read(X)	Reads only X bytes
Line = File2read.readLine()	Reads following line
Lines = File2read.readLins()	Reads the whole file and stores the content in a line strings list
File2write(data)	Writes data in the file
File2write.writeLine(List_line)	Writes in the file the strings line of the list List_line
File2write.close()	Closes the file manually

After you open a file, you have a file data object. Then, its methods can be used in reading and writing with the methods presented in the table above. In either case, the file data object methods take and return only strings in Python. In other words, the read method returns as a data object type as a string.

The write method takes as data object type as string, too. Both methods have different varieties.

The role of the close method is closing the connection between Python and the external file residing in the hardware of your machine. Python also liberates the space in memory that was occupied by an object after it is no longer referenced in the script. Python would also close automatically the close if required. Hence, in Python, it is not necessary to call the close method in order to delete the file object reference manually. However, it is good practice to call the close method after you finish reading or writing a file.

Example File Processing in Python

In this section, we are going to present some examples of processing files in Python using the methods presented in Table 10. The first example illustrates how to write the 'Hello World' in a file. So, let's go back to prompt shell and launch Python for practice.

```
>>> File = open (' MyFile.txt', 'w')
>>> File.write(' Hello World! \n')
>>> File.close()
```

In the first statement, we called the method open in write mode (i.e. 'w') to create the file. The second statement writes the line 'Hello World!' with a newline marker. The third statement closes the file object. In the following code example, we are going to open the file in reading mode (i.e. 'r') and get the line written in the file:

    >>> File = open (' MyFile.txt', 'r')
    >>> A = File.readline()
    >>> print (' This is an example of reading a file with readline: \n', A)
    This is an example of reading a file with readline:
    Hello World!
    >>> File.close()

Now, we are going to add a second line in our file. To do so, we are going to open the file in mode append (i.e. 'a') and write the line 'My first file in Python':

    >>> File = open (' MyFile.txt', 'a')
    >>> File.write(' This is my first file in Python')
    >>> File.close()

If we open the file again and check its content with the read method, we get the following output:

    >>> File = open (' MyFile.txt', 'r')
    >>> A = File.read()
    >>> print (' This is an example of reading a file with read: \n', A)
    This is an example of reading a file with read:
    Hello World!
    This is my first file in Python
    >>> File.close()

As you can notice when opening a file with append mode, it adds whatever you write in the file at the end. We can also change what is already in the file by opening the file in mode 'r+'. When you open the file in this mode and write in it, it will overwrite everything in it. For instance:

>>> File = open (' MyFile.txt', 'r+')
>>> File.write(' This is my first file Python opened in mode r+')
>>> File.close()
>>> File = open (' MyFile.txt', 'r')
>>> A = File.read()
>>> print (' Checking file after opening in mode r+: \n', A)
Checking file after opening in mode r+:
This is my first file Python opened in mode r+
>>>File.close()

Remember, loops are very handy when it comes to repeating the same tasks for a specific number of times. In particular, loops are very useful in processing the file data object. We have seen through the above examples that we can read the content of the whole file in one single step using the read method. In some cases, we need to read the file line by line.

In this case, we would use the readLine method. We might also need to write the file line by line in the case of formatted files, in which case, the writelines is handy. Let's practice some examples. First, we are going to write using writelines method. Then we are going to read the same file line by line. For both tasks, we will use a while loop.

>>> List_string = [' This is an example of \n',
... 'writing a file \n',
... ' on multiple lines\n',
... ' using write Lines \n',
... ' inside a while loop']
>>>print (' List of strings is:\n ', List_string)
List of strings is:
[' This is an example of \n', 'writing a file \n', ' on multiple lines\n', ' using write Lines', ' inside a while loop']
>>> File = open ('Test', 'w')
>>> File.writelines (List_string)
>>> File.close ()

Remember that all file object methods process only strings. Therefore, we created a list of strings where each element end with /n for newline maker.

Now, we open the file for reading:

>>> File = open ('Test', 'r')
>>> while 1:
...   Line = File.readline ()
...   if not Line: break
...   print (Line)
...
This is an example of
writing a file
on multiple lines
using write Lines inside a while loop
>>> File.close ()

As you can notice, we have a break statement in the while loop. This ensures that the while loop stops when there is no line to read. In other words, it ensures that the loop exit when it reaches the end of the file. Because 1 is always evaluated to true, the loop will continue running until it runs to the break. Hence, this loop reads the file line by line until it reaches the end of the file.

If we open the file and use the read method, we get exactly the same results:

```
>>> File = open ('Test', 'r')
>>> A = File.read ()
>>> print ('This is the output from reading the file with reading method: \n', A)
This is the output from reading the file with reading method:
This is an example of
writing a file
on multiple lines
using write Lines inside a while loop
>>> File.close ()
```

Note in this last example, we did not specify the file extension. In fact, Python allows handling and processing any type of files that the extension does not matter. These methods work the same on any file.

Conclusion

Thank you for making it through to the end of *Python Programming: A Comprehensive Smart Approach for Total Beginners to Learn Python Language Using Best Practices And Advanced Features*. Let's hope it was informative and able to provide you with all of the tools you need to achieve your goals whatever they may be.

This book provides the basics of Python language programming. It also covers some advanced topics such as developing modules, debugging, and handling files. This book does not require any programming prerequisites. On the contrary, this book is designed to provide total beginners with the right tools to start programming using the Python language.

In the very first chapters, chapter 1 to chapter 3, we cover the most basics of any programming language which are how to install the language and how to run scripts. We also cover the data object type and how to process them. In chapter 4, we start diving into more details about Python syntax, operators, and if test and loops specifics to process data objects. In the rest of the book, we cover more advanced topics such as developing functions and modules to make any script reusable and widely sharable with others. We also cover debugging which allows finding and fixing code errors, and finally, how to process files. All chapters of this book provide code examples that allow practicing while you are learning the language.

After finishing this book, you will not only be able to develop scripts to accomplish simple tasks, but you will be also able to develop your own modules. You will also be able to use these modules within any program. In short, you will be able to master basic programming with Python with some advanced features. You will also be able to debug and scrutinize your programs while they are running. Once you master these skills, you will be able to pick up more advanced skills easily.

Finally, if you found this book useful in any way, a review on Amazon is always appreciated!

www.ingramcontent.com/pod-product-compliance
Lightning Source LLC
Chambersburg PA
CBHW070624220526
45466CB00001B/86